P9-EDT-576

TABLE OF CONTENTS

THE POWER OF WHO!

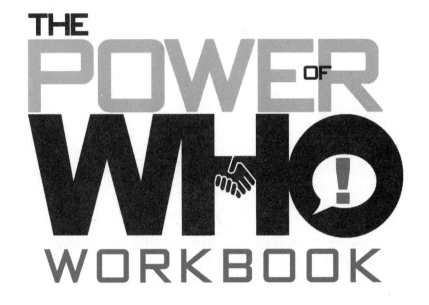

WORKBOOK

BOB BEAUDINE

Eastman-Beaudine
7210 Bishop Street
Suite 220
Plano, Texas 75024

Visit our websites at PowerofWho.com and Eastman-Beaudine.com

The Power of WHO! and *The Power of WHO! Workbook* names and logos are trademarks of Eastman-Beaudine.com

Printed in the United States of America

First Edition: November 2011

ISBN: 978-0-9847-398-0-6

ACKNOWLEDGMENTS

Everyone should write a book. Why? Just so you could write an acknowledgments page. What could be better than to thank your loved ones (your WHO) for all they do and how they help you through this crazy life we live?

Carolyn Castleberry, author/founder of womensavemoney.com and Corey Blake and Nathan Brown of Writers of the Roundtable were there at the beginning. They were a great help and encouragement to me as I started out this journey. I then met Tom Ziglar, Zig's amazing son! Tom was a catalyst by introducing me to Bruce Barbour, a 30 year veteran in the publishing business. Bruce has to be singled out and acknowledged for his encouragement, creativity and wonderful literary skills. He pushed me to take all that I had learned since writing *The Power of WHO* and bring a "fresh insight" to this book. Thanks too for editorial help from Susan Andrews and Jenny Read, and to Bob Bubnis for his creative design. The amazing Power of WHO logo was done by my WHO friend Amber Brown of Visionary Branding.

Big thanks to Dave Ramsey, who's been so supportive of *The Power of WHO* on TV and radio the last two years and now this workbook!

A shout out to my daughters Aly, Rachel & son-in law Donovan, who acted as sounding boards. Special thanks to my other daughter Jenny, who designed the Power of WHO! website and inspired me to write a workbook. To my sister Nancy and my right hand and "clone" Katy who listened, read and gave creative thoughts and encouragement to every draft!

Many WHO Friends need to be acknowledged: Dutch Baughman, Jordan Bazant, Dan Bennett, Robin Blakeley, Jeb Blount, Will Brewer, Tom Chenault, Carlyn Davis, Ray Davis, Jim Donofrio, Dale Dodson, Scott Drew, Todd Duncan, Chester Elton, Jeff Fehlis, Randy Frazee, Rick George, Adrian Gostick, Cheryl Hall, Darren Hardy, Jim Hoffman, Stewart Hunter, Bob Innamorati, Candace Campbell Jackson, June Jones, Mark Kane, Floyd Keith, Greg Kostura, Jim McMahan, Joe Martin, Michael Nadeau, Ed Perrin, Ken Potrock, Mike Reilly,

6 | ACKNOWLEDGMENTS

Dave Savage, Dave Scullin, Grant Teaff, Tom Thomas, Bob Tiede, Cary Turner, Mike Vaught, Mike Wade, Andrew Weightman, Dennis Welch, Doyle & Margorie Whitaker and Richard & Sherry Wright.

To my #1 WHO, a true gift of God, my wife Cheryl. Whose encouragement, support and faith in me sustained me through many a detour. Your love lifts me up!

Finally, to all my WHO Friends that called and sent me letters, met me at speeches, on Facebook, LinkedIn, Google, GA and Twitter! Thank you for endorsing *The Power of WHO*. You inspired me to go deeper and here it is-Your Workbook! May this message of "Doing Life with Friends" transform your life and the lives of those you love!

FOREWORD

Life's fickle, just when you get comfortable with the rhythm of your life, BAM! It changes. But listen closely. **All it takes is just one thought, one idea or one WHO friend and your world can change for the better... in a moment's flash.**

Have you noticed that some messages you're given are so timely and make so much sense, it's as if they were written just for you. They were! Receive the encouragement in this workbook because I believe: "Your Best Is Yet To Be!"

I was asked by a friend, Jay Johnson, to speak to his Henry Wade Juvenile Detention Center kids. He told me there were going to be about forty 16 to 17 year old boys and girls in the room and each one was just one strike away from possibly going to prison. He wanted me to share the message of *The Power of WHO.* I thought to myself as I drove out to the Center, what would I say...? Would these teenagers who had made nothing but bad choices for a long, long time in their young lives understand this concept...? Would they listen to an "old" guy like me? Would they even care...?

HENRY WADE JUVENILE DETENTION CENTER

As I entered this secure facility and walked into the room with these forty young people, I felt all the air go out of my lungs. As I looked around the room, there were four large male adults that looked tough, like guards. My friend Jay wasn't able to be there with me that morning for some reason so someone I didn't know, and who didn't know anything about me or my message, made the introduction. Ugh! He started, "We mentioned to you all that Mr. Beaudine was here to speak to you. I want you to sit up straight in your chairs and give him your full attention. Do I make myself clear?" That was not exactly the introduction I had hoped for…!

For the first several minutes I spoke, I felt like a bad stand up comedian. I had no inspiration and just rambled in search of something that would connect with these kids. I got off base. I let the room's spirit of discouragement, aimlessness, rejection and a total lack of love splash mud all over me. And then…suddenly, I remembered WHO I was, why I was here, and the message I was called to deliver. Nothing was going to stop me from doing it!

I told them, "Today, I believe is going to be a life-changing moment for you if you'll just open your heart to what I am about to say. It's a simple and short message called 'One Friend.'" I asked them all to repeat that phrase, "One Friend." I think, maybe three kids repeated it with me under their breaths! I asked them to raise one finger to the sky and scream it with me. This time, a few more joined me, "One Friend!"

Then I said, "You're here in this room because you chose the wrong one! The wrong friend! Big Mistake! If you haven't figured it out by now, I'm here to tell you that life's about YAWYAW. You know what that means? It means "You Are Who You Associate With." All of a sudden, the kids were no longer slumped in their chairs. I had their attention for the first time.

I then asked Roderick, the toughest kid in the room, "If there was a problem, a crisis, a disaster in this room right now, who would you turn to for help? Who's that 'One Friend'"? He didn't respond at first and then I asked him to stand up and point out that friend to all of us. I said, "Go ahead tell me! Who's the One Friend?" I waited… and then he pointed to a young man across the room. I asked that other young man to stand up. I asked him what his name was and he said Jamal. I said, "Well Jamal, is Roderick your friend?" And he sheepishly smiled and declared, "Yes, he is!" I told Roderick, "Friends are special! They need to be treasured. Go over right now and give your friend a high five!" He did! Slapped his friend's hand hard! I said, "Give-em a hug." The room sighed kind of…ugh. But he did that too! And at that moment, you could just feel the room changed! Hope, encouragement and energy re-entered the room! Now, I was in business!

I asked five or six others to "declare" their One Friend and they all did, until I got to Felipe. He said he had no friends,

"No one to turn to. No one even knows my name." "Well Felipe," I said; "Who would you turn to if you had to? Who is that one person? Tell me your choice, tell me now!" He thought about it and finally pointed to one of the four adults. This guy was big; he had one of those long beards that the members of the band ZZ Top used to have. When he declared that, the adult yelled to him, "Get over here Felipe, I want my hug!" The whole room laughed as he got his hug!

I closed my talk sharing how the power of friendship could change their lives and the lives of those they love. But that there was a price of admission, a code of conduct they must follow. I brought each a gift, a 3x5 card that had the 12 guidelines of friendship on it. If they wanted this, I'd take a moment at the end and sign each one to them personally and listen to their dream if they wanted me to. They all got in line. The card was great but what everyone wants is to share their dream with a friend, with someone who really, honestly and truly cares about them.

That's what this workbook is about. You, learning, thinking and then writing down your goals, your dreams with me here! It all starts with WHO! Finding that "One Friend!" When you do...everything changes for the better!

To the memory of my Dad and Mom, Frank and Martha Beaudine, whose core values, wisdom and love fill the pages of this book. My Dad was my best friend, mentor and partner in business for twenty years. He made coming to work a joy. My mom was the best example of unconditional love I have ever known. I miss you both!

INTRODUCTION

"May you have eyes to see the blessings and wonders right in front of you. May you have ears to hear the sounds of love coming from your family and friends. True friends are treasures. May you treasure the gifts you've been given. And may your eyes be opened to the treasures you've been missing. One final thing, may you polish and condition each of your treasures and cause them to shine."

~Charlie's Blessing

What if I told you that you've been given key relationships in your life, which have been specifically placed there to help you in ways you never imagined? And what if those special people are not just happenstance acquaintances, but are strategic relationships meant to be actively involved in helping you find that place in life you always dreamed about? And, as these relationships are nurtured and nourished over time, you will in turn have the chance to impact their lives in the same way they have touched yours. Is that an incredible thought or what?

Could it be that we've missed the simplicity behind this mysterious thing called destiny? What if the real problem finding that dream job, winning that big piece of business or even getting your mom into the right hospital isn't about relationships you have yet to make, but more about revisiting existing friendships you have unconsciously neglected?

THE SEED OF FRIENDSHIP

I love the parable of the mustard seed. Do you know it? It's about a seed that's smaller than all seeds. But, when it is grown, it is greater than the herbs, and becomes a tree, so that the birds of the air come and lodge in its branches. Yes, this tiniest of all seeds, once planted and cultivated, can yield a very large and flourishing tree that provides a place of rest and refuge for thousands of birds for decades.

This parable is a perfect analogy to our friendships today. What starts out small, over time with the proper nutrition and cultivation, can yield you and me an abundant harvest.

"The Power of WHO" is a message of hope. It is a story of how just 12 friends, 3 close friends and 1 best friend, can unleash a power on your behalf beyond your wildest imagination. It can change the entire trajectory of your life and those you love. The development and cultivation of even one tiny mustard seed, "one friend" is and has always been the missing link we were seeking.

Since writing my first book *The Power of WHO* a few years ago, I am asked time and time again, "Bob, *how* do you WHO?" Whether I am speaking to a group of executives from a Fortune 100 company, a group of athletes, or top officials from major universities, everybody asks for help getting started. With all this in mind, I decided a workbook was the best tool I could provide. So that's what this book is: your WHO resource that will teach you how to live by the "Law of Less," which is a paradigm shift from thinking the secret to fulfillment and success is having thousands of friends, fans and followers to spending more time with less people and building deep relationships with close WHO friends.

I want you to put these next three special words deep in your heart as you work through this workbook. The three words are: "I'm Not Alone!" That's what I learned while writing *The Power of WHO,* finding an agent, a publisher and even getting on The Today Show, CNBC and Dave Ramsey. And the good news is "Neither Are You" in your search for your goals and dreams! You see, what you're about to discover in this workbook is: You Got WHO! You have a community of friends, just like I did, that will come to your aid if you'll only ask them. But it's the Remembering, Reaching Out, and Reconnecting with these "gifts" in life that is going to be the real work of this workbook. I'm excited, I hope you are too—Let's get started!

CHAPTER 1

FRIENDS VS. ACQUAINTANCES

"People walk around today calling everyone their best friend. The term doesn't have any real meaning anymore. Mere acquaintances are lavished with hugs and kisses upon a second or, at most, a third meeting. Birthday cards get passed around the office so everybody can scribble a snippet of sentimentality for a colleague they have barely met. And everybody just loves everyone. As a result, when you tell someone you love someone today, it isn't much heard."
~Alan Shore/Denny Crane-Boston Legal

Do yourself an enormous favor. Don't make the potentially painful mistake of fantasizing that someone is your friend when, in fact, they are merely a friendly acquaintance. There's a few light-years' distance between "friendly" and "friend." Social mega-network Facebook has redefined the boundaries of friendship. Gone are the days of saying someone is a "friend" and that meant you had a living, breathing face to face relationship with the person. Today, we can be "friends" with people we've never met. That's why I couldn't name my original book *The Power of Friendship* because I had 4,700 plus people on Facebook that were my "friend!" No, I had to come up with a new name for what people call their "friends" and that's how I came up with your "WHO!" The people "WHO" matter most in your life!

But recognizing these true friends (your WHO) from the myriad of acquaintances that crowd around our life is a difficult task. Why? Because friendship has been redefined in our culture to mean something less than what it actually is. We've all heard people say something like, "Oh, I've got lots of friends!" No, they don't.

Not really. Such a person has no concept that real friendship requires intimacy, depth and commitment. You can't have "lots of friends" because no one has the time or emotional space to be close friends with more than just a few. In business this is also common. They say: "I know Bob Beaudine." Really? What's his wife's name? Have you been over to his house for a barbeque?

Surprisingly, most people I talk to haven't given much thought to the varying dynamics involved in their relationships so there might be some confusion. So, to better help you differentiate your "WHO friends" from the rest of your database of "so-called friends" I've written "12 Guidelines of True Friendship." Let's look at them.

A TRUE FRIEND...

1. **Gives unconditional LOVE- Is someone who simply loves you for no good reason, no strings attached. They will do their best to help you- Just Because.**

2. **Will try to help you right now. When you call for help, the answer is "YES!" An acquaintance merely wishes you well.**

3. **Wants you to succeed and seeks to empower you as you pursue your dream.**

4. **Is a chisel helping you to carve away those areas in your life that hold you back from fulfilling your dream.**

5. **Holds you accountable to your stated goals. They have earned an ALL ACCESS Backstage Pass to your life.**

6. **Is someone who knows the song in your heart and can sing it back to you when you have forgotten the words.**

7. **Has no ulterior motive and is always loyal, always on your side, always "true blue" all the way through.**

8. **Is a trusted Secret Keeper—Knows you well enough to know your secrets and keep them. And you know their character well enough to know they will never betray you.**

9. Has forged an indelible impression on your heart and soul that has altered your life in a positive way.

10. Brings out the best in you and shares your core values, the important pillars that support your life.

11. Will go out of their way to do things for you that would never cross the mind of a mere friendly acquaintance.

12. Doesn't need you to be anybody other than who you are, but is glad to see you become something more.

As you look at this list above ask yourself: Is this the kind of friend you are?

List the names of people coming to your mind that have these qualities of friendship with you.

_____

_____

_____

_____

_____

_____

_____

_____

_____

_____

_____

_____

_____

_____

_____

_____

There has to be a price of admission for friendship, doesn't there? I have always heard, that success was 80% just showing up. But if that's true, then "showing up" is especially true when talking about friendships. James Taylor's poetic lyrics are spot-on when it comes to the most important quality of a true friend: "You just call out my name and, you know wherever I am, ... I'll be there...you've got a friend."

Being there.
The essence
of friendship.

Have you noticed that TRUE friends always find great fulfillment in helping each other? In fact, they come pre-wired with a strong desire to help us. I saw this firsthand recently when my daughter got stuck at an airport coming home from college. In a panic, she called me and I immediately reached out for help from a

WHO friend who works at the airline. I told him my dilemma that Rachel might not be able to get home for her grandparents 60th wedding anniversary. He immediately said: "I've got you covered my friend—don't worry. I'll get her home on time!" I told him: "I hope I'm not asking too much" and he interrupted me saying: "Bob, what are you talking about? It's a 'WHO Honor' to help you and your daughter! That's what The Power of WHO is all about, isn't it? Friends helping friends!" "Yes," I said thankfully! Wow! A WHO Honor! How good is that?!

You see, whether it's a reference, an endorsement or a testimonial for a large piece of business/dream job you're seeking or on the home front or helping you find a babysitter, doctor, or tickets to that special event, there is a big difference between asking friends or acquaintances for help. It usually comes down to this: "Friends help you now and acquaintances… just wish you well."

> In order to have a friend, you and I both understand you must BE a friend.

Perhaps you already enjoy this type of mutual friendship with a few people. If so, name them in the spaces below:

1. _____

2. _____

3. _____

In what ways are you a friend to others?

_____

_____

_____

_____

_____

_____

_____

_____

_____

_____

_____

Do you have any friends whose number comes up on the caller ID and you wrestle with whether or not to answer the call? Write their names below.

1. _____

2. _____

3. _____

Thinking about your top three friendships. List ways you are each person's friend.

1. _____

2. _____

3. _____

Now would be a good time to review what you've written down thus far. Ask yourself a few questions to get your mind working:

- Who has influenced and affected you by their friendship over the years?
- Who calls you regularly to see how you're doing?
- Who invests in your friendship?
- Who picks you up when you're down and out?
- Who do you trust in times of crisis?
- Who keeps you accountable?
- Who celebrates you?

Next, list specific ways you maintain/nourish your friendship with each.

1. _____

2. _____

3. _____

I believe we're given friends in life purposely, intentionally for not only our mutual enjoyment and fulfillment, but to help guide and empower us to utilize our gifts and talents to their highest cause. The key is 12 friends, 3 who are close and 1 who is your best friend. These special 12 individuals have a much greater influence on your life and future destiny than you ever imagined. They may or may not be activated yet in your day-to-day journey, but they are there. And together, we're going to discover these special "gifts" in this workbook.

Remember: each of these 12 friends possess different qualities and characteristics that make them unique and important to you. **No one person's friendship can** **provide you all you need.** So stop getting upset at your mate when they aren't the compassionate giver or encourager you need at the time. You might always be that to them and want them to reciprocate, but that's not what their gift is to you. That's why we need the 12! Some are: extroverted motivators; others quietly discerning. Some

"Tee you up," promote you, sing your praises and introduce you for business/jobs/ social gatherings better than anyone else you've ever known. One of these 12 is your closest companion/running buddy. They love doing/going/sharing what you love doing. One of these is your "Secret Keeper," the one you approach when you need the truth and another when you need a shoulder to lean on. Some will provide a realistic perspective, while others will help you dream bigger. Discovering these 12 friends is as vital to your dreams as food and water are to your bodies.

So try this exercise. I've already asked you to think of 3 friends. Transfer these names to the list below and then name 9 more. This time, however, as you make your list, think about your top 3 friends and that 1 very best friend.

1. _____

2. _____

3. _____

4. _____

5. _____

6. _____

7. _____

8. _____

9. _____

10. _____

11. _____

12. _____

These names may not be the same ones you listed previously. That's okay. Your spouse/mate should make your 12, but may not be in your top 3; this is also okay and not a betrayal. Your friends will never be in the same covenant relationship with you as your spouse, but your spouse may not share your same interests or hobbies—which is why the phrase "opposites attract" is so true of many marriages.

Now, you may not think you have 12 true friends who fit these characteristics, but I assure you, you do—or will. Like the mustard plant which began with the tiniest seed, every relationship needs to be maintained and nourished to grow. In the coming chapters, we'll work together to help you identify relationships you already have that, with just a little cultivation/development, can bloom into beautiful, healthy and long-lasting friendships. We'll also talk about how to maintain these healthy relationships you presently have and not allow them to wither on the vine. And finally, we'll discuss ways to rejuvenate past friendships that somehow-- life, circumstances, time or distance-- may have separated.

In the next chapter, I will walk you through "the Wilderness Journey." I will discuss why it's so important to

Wanted: Friend
Prospective candidates will:

Allow me to be myself, and love me for it

Affirm my best qualities (especially when I am feeling insecure)

Call out the best in me, and hold me accountable to the best version of myself

Listen without judging or trying to fix me

Give me the benefit of the doubt

Give me a break when I am grumpy or having a bad day

Know what I like

Love me regardless of my past

Spend time with me, just because they enjoy my company

Speak well of me when I am not in the room

Speak the truth to me when no one else will

Never shame me, diminish me, or make me feel small

Become excited about what I am excited about

Celebrate my victories!

go and how to do it the right way step by step. Before you think you need to book a flight to Wyoming or Montana in order to discover your "wilderness," let me define what I mean. The purpose of a Wilderness Journey is to set aside a significant time of solitude and reflection to create a powerful, liberating space in which you're able to:

- Quiet your mind
- Dream again
- Discover your "WHO, WHAT, WHERE, WHEN and WHY?"
- Rediscover what makes you feel fulfilled, satisfied, and content
- Reevaluate where your gifts and talents should be applied
- Think deeply about the impact you would like your life to make on others
- Plan the LEGACY you wish to leave

Those of us who go on a Wilderness Journey discover new realities that previously we were unaware even existed. In fact, a trip like this will surprise you sometimes with something so wonderful you can't believe it. So get ready and start looking with an expectant, hope-filled heart and you'll encounter some things that will have a deep, restorative effect.

CHAPTER 2

YOUR WILDERNESS JOURNEY

"Your vision will become clear only when you look into your heart. He who looks outside—dreams, he who looks inside... awakens." —Carl Jung

I can't tell you how many times as a CEO of an executive search firm I've listened to someone say they desperately wanted to get from point A to point B, but had no clue how to get there. So what do they do? Well, they don't know what to do, so they... wait. And while they're waiting, they continue doing the same old things they have always done but hoping for different results. Surprisingly, **I've discovered that individuals who are willing to make even a few slight course corrections were able to alter the entire trajectory of their lives.** At first, a lot of these people thought they needed an extreme makeover, but the good news is that just a small change in strategy makes all the difference.

What's the strategy? It's simple. You need some time alone—time alone with yourself, with nature and God. This time of solitude and reflection is what's needed. (The "looking inside" part is implied in the "solitude and reflection.") It's what I refer to as your "Wilderness Journey." Taking time away—for yourself, by yourself—is the best prescription I can write for your mental, emotional, physical, and possibly, spiritual health. Doing so creates a powerful, liberating space in which you're able to rediscover WHO you are, what you want and what matters most.

But, unfortunately for most people, taking "time-out" is the last thing they feel they can do. In fact, they come up with lots of excuses of why they can't get away:

- I'm too busy.
- My spouse/boss would never let me.
- I'm too late; I missed my opportunity; I'm too young/too old; too whatever...
- What if I go out there and come back with nothing?
- I can do it as I drive to work in the morning.

I urge you the first time you go on a Wilderness Journey that you actually GO away from your home and familiar surroundings for three days to a place where you can be alone with your thoughts.

What's the point of getting away and being quiet?

To disengage from the routine and chaos of life to consider:

- WHO am I?
- WHAT's my destiny?
- What makes me full of joy and peace?
- What (or who) stresses me out?
- How do I do more of the things that give me joy and peace and less of what stresses me out?
- How will I develop a discipline of solitude and learn to be comfortable with being alone with myself?
- How will I listen to what I'm saying?
- How will I develop a plan to Remember, Reach Out and Reconnect with significant people in my life?

Where do I go? Well, that's up to you. Each of us gets inspired differently. Some like the ocean, the mountains, or the forest. Some like to be out at a lake or at a stream. The odds are that one of your WHO probably has a place or knows of a place through family/friends that they would love to let you use or point you to. But if you feel you don't have that option, there are other places nearby to seek solitude:

- Get a tent and camp out.
- Head out to a hotel in a quiet place out of town.
- Stay at a state park lodge.
- Anywhere that is quiet.

If you can get away for several days, that would be ideal. But even if you spent just one day without distractions in a quiet place like a nearby park, a local hotel courtyard, or beside a neighborhood man-made lake—it would be a good start.

What do I take with me when I go?

☐ iPod, smartphone or mp3 to listen to soothing music. Download Pandora or Jazz Radio for easy listening or inspirational music. Your goal is to create a relaxed atmosphere.

☐ Database of names/Contact Manager on smartphone, tablet or laptop. Do not take this to check email, surf the web or work! It's only there to review all the people (your WHO) in your address book.

- *The Power of WHO* book as a reference.
- Legal Pad and lots of pencils with extra erasers!

☐ Spiritual or Inspirational books. Not a novel for entertainment!

Where do I start?

☐ First, get settled wherever you are. Have the right comfortable clothes, shoes, and chair.

☐ The goal is to quiet your mind so you can begin to think reflectively.

☐ Visualize doing something that totally relaxes you.

☐ Don't rush this first day. If you doze off—great. Maybe you needed it.

☐ Just sit and think.

☐ Enjoy an activity which promotes relaxation, such as reading, meditating, or watching a good sunset—any pastime to get you off the treadmill of anxiety found in everyday life.

☐ Verbalize your goals for the next few hours. Write them down here.

☐ Tell God you're here and ready to listen! Pray for His guidance/ direction/answers over the next few days.

☐ Now, meditate, reflect and listen to your self-talk. What are you saying? Is it positive? If yes, good. If the thought is negative ("I don't like being alone", "I don't hear anything", or "I don't deserve to be happy or pursue my dream"), write down what you're feeling and what you're going to do to turn this negative thinking around.

Make a list of the favorite things you did when you were younger. Go as far back as you can recall. How many of those same things are you doing now? How often? What would you need to do differently to be able to do these things again and more frequently?

What did people say you were really good at when you were younger? And more recently? Are you still doing those things? If so, good! If not, why not?

_____

_____

_____

_____

_____

_____

What could you be doing at home, work, in your community, with your friends and family that would be enjoyable and fulfilling?

_____

_____

_____

_____

_____

_____

What are the elements of success? How are you actively engaged at work, at home, or in your community? Who do you share these experiences with most frequently?

_____

_____

_____

_____

_____

_____

_____

Define who your friends have been over the years. Check that address book to remind yourself of good times you've had with friends you may not have seen or thought about lately.

_____

_____

_____

_____

_____

_____

Make a list of the family/friends you have in your life right now that encourage you.

_____

_____

_____

_____

_____

_____

_____

Who was in your life in years past that you really loved but haven't talked to in a while? Why? How can you Reconnect?

_____

_____

_____

Who makes you laugh? Whose energy do you need at least once a day?

_____

_____

_____

Who do you call in a crisis? Write below a person you feel is a Secret Keeper. This person has wisdom and cares about you.

_____

Who are the cheerleaders of your life? They introduce you well and always say nice things about you to others.

_____

_____

_____

Who are your accountability partners? These people have wisdom and care about you.

_____

_____

_____

Who has given you an endorsement, testimonial, a reference? Who has recommended you for jobs over the years?

_____

_____

_____

Make a list 10-20 people who you could call and invite to lunch or coffee.

_____   _____

_____   _____

_____   _____

_____   _____

_____   _____

_____   _____

_____   _____

_____   _____

_____   _____

From this list, are there 12 people who might be closer than the others? Define those you think are closer and why.

_____   _____

_____   _____

_____   _____

_____   _____

_____   _____

Of that group of 12, are there 3 or 4 who you know you can count on? These people would be there for you if you called and you would do the same for them.

_____

_____

_____

_____

Is there 1 person on that list of WHO you can trust above all others? Someone you can share your dreams, your fears, and your challenges with?

_____

And, here is what you do when you get home:

1. Decide to "declare" your friendship to these 12 by telling them how much they mean to you.

2. Develop an action plan for each one over the next few months. Even the slightest bit of attention will reap great rewards of a deeper friendship. Be attentive and active.

3. Reflect on your dreams, your personal destiny, your new goals and your action plan to Reconnect with your close friends.

Remember that this mountain top experience must now be put into action in the fields and valleys of everyday life and work. Remember the discipline of solitude that you enjoyed and make time to take time every morning to listen and reflect on your new priorities. Armed with your action plan, you are now ready to connect your WHO to your WHAT. You already know someone right now who knows the right person who will help you achieve your goals, or someone who can introduce you to just the right person you need to meet.

If I challenged you to stop right now and refocus your efforts on pursuing a lifelong dream, or even a short-term goal, what would it be?

_____

Once you answer that question, I have two more:
Who would you call for assistance?

_____

How many WHOs would you call?

_____

These are some of the questions I want you to reflect on. You'll have a lot of your own as well. Write down those thoughts here.

_____

_____

_____

I heard it said once that you could become blind by seeing each day as one and the same. In many ways, that could be true—but what a waste that would be! I see each day as a new gift! A wonderful adventure with many twists and turns along the path. But we must pay attention to the clues. That's what this Wilderness Journey will do for you if you'll give it a chance. It's a significant exercise and discipline toward living the life you've dreamed.

There are millions of people who will never do this, so they remain stuck where they are. They're not willing to take the risk of being alone with just their thoughts, or they don't really believe they'll discover anything new. Don't be part of that crowd. It's a dead end. A "time-out" right now could keep you from getting stuck for several more years in a job, relationship, or just another situation that leads to another dead end. When you rediscover what makes you feel fulfilled, satisfied and content, you will have accomplished something very significant. **Let's Go!**

CHAPTER 3

THE DISCOVERY

"For I know the plans I have for you," declares the LORD, "plans to prosper you and not to harm you, plans to give you hope and a future." —Jeremiah 29:11

I had just come off the stage having given a talk to the "Black Coaches Association" on "The Power of WHO" when one of the coaches asked me for a private moment. His opening line was "Did you just do that talk for me?" I said, "Probably" with a slight chuckle. He said, "Well, you have to hear my WHO story!"

"I've been defensive coordinator for a team for a number of years. Before that I traipsed my wife and kids around the country from team to team, not sure if I'd ever get chance to settle down. My wife always dreamed of me being a head coach in her hometown. Her parents hadn't seen much of their grandkids and she was homesick. So when the job came open, I immediately sent in my resume/video. I also logged online and filled out the information that the university required. But I was worried about my chances since I didn't know anyone at the school, and I hadn't heard one lick from them since submitting my information.

"After a few days, I finally told my wife about the job opening. 'Oh my gosh,' she said. 'You've got to get that position! It's perfect!' She was so hopeful and excited, but I was more reserved. I said, 'It does seem perfect, and I've done all I could do to get the job, but unfortunately I don't think that's enough.' She got quiet and then said, 'I just read a book.' 'Huh?' I said. 'It's called *The Power of WHO*" she said. I said 'Great...' sarcastically. 'Is that like that Tony Robbins' stuff?' She ignored my remark and said,

'The book had this amazing line: You already know everyone you need to know!' I said: 'What does that mean?' She said: 'It means what if I told you that my dad knows someone at the university who could help you. Would you want me to ask him?'

My first thought was, 'No, I don't want my father-in-law's help!' But... as I was lying there in bed with no other real alternatives, I said, 'Yes, sure, ask him!'"

He then shared that the next day his father-in-law called. He said, "Son, would you like me to reach out on your behalf?" With that question I was thinking, "How could I grab the knife out of my back," but he told me he resisted that line of thinking and asked his father-in-law, "Who do you know at the school?" The father-in-law said, "I've worked out with a guy at Gold's Gym for a year or so and we've become pretty good friends. I know he is involved there." The coach immediately thought, "You've got to be kidding me, this is what everyone was talking about? A guy you workout with?" But, once again he held back what he was thinking and said, "What's his name, I'll look him up on the computer." When my father-in-law gave me the name, it came up that he was the Chairman of the University Board of Regents. Wow! With just one call from my father-in-law to his workout buddy on my behalf, something magical and powerful happened: I immediately got an interview. I am now the Head Coach!! "So let me get this straight," he said to me. "All along laying right there next to me was my answer, my WHO. And I had never thought to ask her for help. What a lesson that was!"

"Yes" I told him, "a lesson for all of us!"

Listen, if you really want to pursue a worthy goal or make a significant change in your life, you don't need to go external in your approach, you must go internal. Here's what most people do: they start looking outside their WHO network thinking their success will be found "out there" somewhere. It's a false notion to think that your success will come from a bunch of people you don't know. Here's the most amazing thing:

"You **Already Know** Everyone You Need To Know!"

You may be saying, "Is that possible?" Yes, it is!

Unfortunately, past generations have lived by the John Wayne/Lone Ranger philosophy, "To truly make it in life, son, you have to go it alone." Or, another well-oiled phrase, "Pull yourself up by your own bootstraps." Its intended meaning is "'to better oneself unaided by one's own efforts; improve your situation by your own efforts."

Have you ever stopped to think about or visualize this phrase? It's impossible to literally pull yourself up by your own bootstraps. No, The Lone Ranger—and his bootstraps—need to be left in the dust because that's not how we were designed to live. You and I—we need each other! No man is an island. We all know deep down that the real value of life is when we come alongside others to accomplish a common goal.

King Solomon was considered "the wisest man who ever lived." He observed, "Two are better than one, because they have a good return for their work; if one falls down, his friend can help him up. But pity the man who falls and has no one to help him up" (Ecclesiastes 4:9-10 NIV).

> **No man is an island! There is great value when we come alongside others to accomplish a common goal.**

The point is clear. Whether it's coaches, teachers, mentors, parents, friends, or neighbors, we need our WHO to help and advise us.

The problem with networking, as people practice it today, is that it implies friendship with people who are only mere acquaintances. As I mentioned, people have been taught—incorrectly—that friends and business do not mix. So let me get this straight, we're supposed to work with people we don't know and don't trust? Because of Ponzi schemes and Madoff shenanigans we are now supposed to disclose our friendships as evil instead of declare them as great! Think again!

I've developed a database of more than 5,365 people in my business world that can say, "Hi, Bob." That really doesn't mean a lot except that I know a lot of people because of my business. I had what I thought was a great networking strategy, but I was about to discover I was dead wrong. I used to try to touch more than 1,000 people a year with notes and calls and visits. It was exhausting!

One day, I stopped and studied who of those 5,365 people had actually touched my life in some significant way over the last 10 years. I can't tell you how shocked I was to learn that there were only 87 out of 5,365! How could I have missed that? My strategy was to run all over the country, giving out little pieces of Bob to thousands of people and the return, in actual business, was nil.

Don't get me wrong. I enjoy meeting people, but I should have been spending more time focusing on and investing in the 87 who were actually impacting my life in significant ways. Yes, I should have!

These 87 incredible people that have had such an impact on my life were friends, relatives, business associates and clients. The common connection we share is a special bond that if I tried, I couldn't adequately explain it with words. I am not unique. You have these same special bonds with people in your life, too. It's this mystical bond that creates a desire to help and support each other. Let me say it again: we all have those special connections.

Now, I focus the majority of my time interacting with my WHO, the people who have impacted my life in significant ways. This means I,

- Spend quality time with the people who truly know and like me.
- Take the time and effort to help these friends accomplish their goals and dreams.
- Ask these friends for help and guidance when I need a helping hand.

I know your question before you ask it. "But, Bob, isn't it a bad idea to mix business and pleasure?" My answer to this question may be over-simplified, but the same answer exists if you asked me if the white and yolk can be separated from an egg once they've been scrambled. Simply, "No." There need not be a business/pleasure difference. This is about "doing life" with the people you care deeply about, who also happen to care deeply about you. You desire their life-success; they desire yours. My dad had a simple mission statement for our firm, Eastman & Beaudine, and we still live to this statement some 40 plus years later. Here it is:

> # MAKE FRIENDS!
>
> ## HELP YOUR FRIENDS IN EVERY WAY POSSIBLE.
>
> ## DON'T BE SURPRISED WHEN YOU DO A LOT OF BUSINESS WITH YOUR FRIENDS!

As I look back in business over the last 30 years, I have discovered all my greatest successes in business came through relationships—deep friendships! Not through cold calls, mass emails, or handing out business cards to strangers. No, it came through people that knew me, trusted me, over years. They knew my gifts and talents, and, yes, liked me. Of course I had to be qualified, but when it came down to me or someone they didn't know, I got the opportunity to shine. To show how much I cared. And I didn't let them down. Wouldn't you work harder for a friend? Yes, of course you would!

We have been created and designed for relationships. Your network of friends is one of the most important components of your life. But be careful here. Don't make the mistake of thinking you need a whole new network of friends in order to be successful. Remember, you already know everyone you need to know to get where you want to go.

Each of us has a WHO network. However, we may have let some of our WHOs slip away and we need to Reconnect with these once-special friends.

Implementing the three **R's** of WHO

Remember

Reach Out

Reconnect

In *The Power of WHO*, I introduced the concept that you have a powerful network of friends which consists of many layers. It starts with your Inner Circle, and expands to your WHO friends. Rounding out your spheres of influence are Allies, Advocates, Acquaintances and Fans. For this chapter, we'll focus on the first circle where your truest friends live.

The "Inner Circle" (12-3-1). Your very closest friends make up your Inner Circle. I tell everyone that you get 12 great friends in life and out of these 12 are 3 close friends and that 1 special best friend. There is a heart connection with these key people, like my wife who occupies my #1 WHO spot.

Your Inner Circle consists of friends who:

- just 'get you' and you 'get them'.
- understand you to the very core of your person.
- love you unconditionally-"Just Because."

A WHO FRIEND

- Calls a halt to fearful thinking by insisting you stop listening to negative self-talk.
- Speaks truth about your value, worth, uniqueness, accomplishments, and your values and dreams.
- Intercepts you when you're wandering down the wrong path and redirects your steps towards a better future.
- Loves and cares about you—unconditionally.
- Knows your true identity and won't let you forget it.

Your closest friends are your Inner Circle of greatest influence.

If you completed the Wilderness Experience, now would be a good time to look back over the names you recorded there. Make revisions if needed, and then transfer this list to the spaces on the next page.

If you have not already identified your 12, take a moment to start writing names down now. This is your book! (Do this first in pencil)

1. _____

2. _____

3. _____

4. _____

5. _____

6. _____

7. _____

8. _____

9. _____

10. _____

11. _____

12. _____

My experience is that very few people of any age have stopped to map out their own network. They miss the latent goodwill, power, and influence that can be unleashed in both their personal and professional lives, as well as for those they love.

You need to consider: with whom you are connected, with whom you are currently doing life? To whom are you providing friendship, value, service and love?

There is power and influence here beyond your dreams. These "12-3-1" have not been given to you by chance. So we have to start treating them with a different code of conduct. (Review 12 rules of friendship on page 14-15.)

Your goals and dreams lay dormant in these untapped connections.

Better relationships
+
Deeper friendships
=
Success.

It's Simple—People Matter Most. Our heart knows it, God teaches it, but somehow over time we forget. And when we do, we lose the Power. We must choose to go deep!

A compelling future awaits you as you discover, develop and maintain these 12 crucial friendships.

CHAPTER 4

A SIMPLE AND EFFECTIVE WAY TO "NETWORK!"

"Help! I need Somebody. Help! Not just Anybody."
– The Beatles

Today, you and I have to "network" for pretty much everything we need and desire in life. For doctors, dentists, new clients, schools, lawyers, mates/dates, babysitters, jobs, hospitals, tickets, and promotions—the list is endless. But **the value for understanding "how to network" the right way is the key to it all!** Knowing this can provide you the "Power" to help you achieve your goals and dreams a whole lot quicker and much more successfully than you could ever imagine.

Now you might be a genius in some areas of your life, but you're going to need others to assist you where you're not so strong. Each of us comes to a chasm in our life and business sooner or later that we can't cross without someone's help. So get over it! Going at it alone is like trying to speed walk on the moon. It's hard to get traction. Conversely, tapping into your "True Authentic Network" is like walking on one of those people-movers at the airport. You just step on and all of a sudden there's a power underneath transporting you to your destination faster than you could get there by yourself. You see, people are "bridges" you must cross to get where you want to go. They serve as catalysts. By definition, a catalyst is an agent that speeds up a process, sometimes exponentially. Now, you can stay on the other side if you choose, but you need to understand that your WHAT will never come into play until your WHO brings you across.

The lyrics from The Beatles hit song "Help!" speaks to a basic need at our very core. In one form or another, on some days more than others, we all need

"Help!" You've most certainly heard the phrase, especially as it applies to finding employment, "It's not what you know, but who you know and who knows you." You may even believe in that or have experienced the truth behind that phrase. But I'm going to encourage you to tweak your thinking here some. Because it's not just "Any WHO" that will do. Like the song implies, it's a very specific WHO you'll need. And knowing WHO these special "somebodies" are in our life is the difference!

The WHO that will help you is:

- *Somebody who* cares about your dream
- *Somebody who* shares your passion
- *Somebody who* has the power and willingness to help you
- *Somebody who* is reliable
- *Somebody who* is willing to take the time and effort to invest in you and assist you any way they can
- *Somebody who* personally knows you and likes you for who you are

Each somebody you already know today can personally link you to another and to another until you see the opportunity you were meant to follow and accomplish. Do not miss the word "personally." This type of people-to-people linking is not to be confused with modern networking (aka "not-working"). Networking is a misunderstood term today because it implies friendship with people who are, in reality, only mere acquaintances at best.

Over many years working with hundreds of clients, our firm developed the incredibly simple, but effective, networking paradigm we call the "100/40 Strategy." This approach puts 'networking' back where it was meant to be—surrounded by our closest friends and their concentric circles of friends. Some call it **"Six Degrees of Separation meets your Dream."** When you employ this strategy, a successful outcome is a foregone conclusion.

The numbers 100/40 matter less than the overall concept. The first set of numbers (up to 100) is all about identifying relationships—your WHO. The second set (up to 40) is about identifying whatever it is you are after—your WHAT. At any point along your life journey the number of your WHO and WHAT can be very different. WHO will be your preeminent, somewhat-fixed, priority list—WHAT will be the list that experiences wider variances.

WHO (1-100)

Most of us don't even think about our closest friends helping us dream, discover, pursue, or accomplish our dreams and goals. Instead, we send resumes to and ask advice from complete strangers. We "network" in the same fashion, passing business cards during boring association meetings usually among people who are vying for the same types of positions or clients. These people don't really care about you and will dispose of your card the minute they get back to their office.

We've compartmentalized our lives into 'personal' versus 'professional'—two mutually exclusive entities that shall not cross paths.

What are the possibilities that would exist if your professional life and personal life were intertwined? Now we're talking!

From my years of experience with the 100-WHO/40-WHAT Strategy, the possibilities are endless!

I love the simplicity and profoundness of Dr. Seuss. In the book and movie, *The Grinch Who Stole Christmas*, it is the strength, determination and love of the entire Whoville community that turns the Grinch's stone-cold heart into a fully-beating heart of love. Dr. Seuss understood The Power of WHO and the great things that happen when a WHO network is put to work for the betterment of one.

We each have our own Whoville (and many of us didn't have to use a dog as a reindeer to get there). Visualize your WHO-community. What's it look like?

We've all heard the phrase "sphere of influence." Your WHO world consists of several spheres as illustrated here. Like ripples in a pond, these spheres will help you to see The Power of WHO in action. You have your own special sphere of influence. As we work through each sphere, you will begin to identify and clarify the various dynamics of others' lives that touch yours. When you begin to understand how this powerful force works within interconnecting circles, you also begin to see how you can interact with these relational circles in ways that greatly benefit your life and the lives of others.

First Step: REMEMBER

This exercise may produce strong emotions—even regret—but stick with it. I promise, clarifying your WHO will only help you as you refocus your time, energy and resources toward more productive and fulfilling means. Hear me—there is a group of people who love you and who want to help you succeed in life. You won't remember all of them today, and don't be discouraged if you can only list a few to begin with. The key is to Just Begin!

Start today to identify your WHO. Make a List!

- People you've really clicked with over the years.
- Not just powerful and influential names.
- I had 87 on my list and I probably wished qualities on 20 or so of them; you might only have 40 or maybe even 20. It's not the quantity-it's the quality that counts!
- People, who if they called and asked you for help, you would do it immediately and ask for nothing in return. These are your WHO and are just special to you.
- Remember the 3R's—Remember, Reach Out, and Reconnect!

Each person that makes your list of WHO friends must share your core values. The only factors keeping them from being in your Inner Circle friends are proximity, opportunity and time. Shared experiences take all three and Inner Circle friends like to do things together. At this point, just write down these names, but don't call them yet. Don't worry—we're just beginning!

SO HOW DO YOU WHO?

Print lists of people with whom you're connected on Facebook, LinkedIn, Twitter, and Google Groups. Look at your database of names on your computer, neighborhood lists, alumni lists, church directories, etc.

Categorize these people into the six different spheres of influence.

Use a pencil to write these names into the categories listed on the next several pages. Out to the side of each name record how you know the person.

My 100 WHO Friends

Where do I find WHO friends? REMEMBER...!

- Grade School/High School friends
- College friends (roommate, dorm mate, sports teammates, fraternity/ sorority brothers/sisters, club/association members, classmates)
- Coworkers and ex-coworkers/Ex-Bosses and ex-employees
- Church friends
- Neighbors
- Workout friends (gym)
- Sports friends (golf, tennis, bowling, basketball, racquetball, softball, etc.)
- Parents of your children's friends
- Family members (yes, including your In-laws)
- Club members (Masons, Choir, Veterans, Harley Davidson friends, etc.)
- Personal health and legal associations (lawyer, dentist, accountant, veterinarian, pharmacist, personal trainer, etc.) Some of these folks may like you enough to want to spend time with you.

YOUR WHO WORLD IS BROKEN INTO SIX SPHERES:

Inner Circle—12-3-1

We discussed your Inner Circle in the previous chapter. These are your top 12 WHO friends. They share a "heart connection" that you just don't have with other people. Of all the people that could possibly affect you, it's these 12 that have the maximum influence in your life. Some of these friends may be near in proximity to you, some live far away. Distance with these friends means nothing. You love them and they love you. The moment you talk to them you are on enhanced mode and you are in tune with the moment at hand. Within this Inner Circle of 12, there are 3 who are your 3 closest friends. They know everything about you and love you anyway. You communicate almost every day and share your life with these individuals. Then there is the 1 best friend with whom you share the deepest kinship. This friend's heart is knit with yours and knows you more intimately that any other friend. Having one of these makes life worth living!

As you progress through this workbook you may think of more people who either presently fit the 12-3-1 profile, or have fit that profile in the past. When you do, record their names below.

_____

_____

_____

_____

_____

_____

"WHO"
FRIENDS

INNER CIRCLE
12
3
1

"WHO Friends"

WHO friends are a natural extension of your Inner Circle. These are people who are special to you and you are special to them. They came into your life for a reason or a season. You might have been getting really close to becoming Inner Circle friends with a few of these over the years, when "poof" they moved to Boise! Ouch! Has that happened to you? I'm sure it has, but did you think you were supposed to stop communicating with them? No! Time, distance and opportunity may separate you, but you still have this connect and desire to keep each other close at hand. That's a clue! Don't miss it! Stay in touch! How? Social networking, cell phones, Skype, and vacations can keep these friends close knit. These friendships are very important. The "Power of WHO" resides in Inner Circle/Who friends!

_____

_____

_____

_____

_____

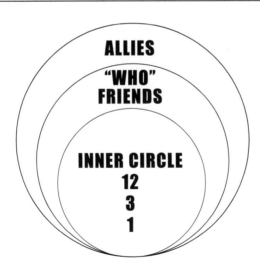

ALLIES

"WHO" FRIENDS

INNER CIRCLE
12
3
1

Allies

"Allies" are people you associate with, connect with, or touch through your 12-3-1 and WHO friends. This is where your WHO circles can begin to really overlap. When your WHO friends open up their WHO world to you, you have now been given access to a whole new group of quality people, each of whom has their own WHO world.

My daughter Aly's good friend Ilana overheard a conversation between Aly and me where Aly was seeking my advice about her aspirations and goals. Once Aly and Ilana were alone, Ilana broke down and shared how much she missed her dad who had passed away a few years prior and really missed having that type of conversation with him. She was concerned about her trip the next week to L.A. to look for a job because she only had one interview set up.

She needed advice but didn't know what to do. Aly boldly said, "No problem… Power of WHO!" "What?" Ilana said. "Power of WHO!" Aly responded. "What's that?" Ilana Asked with a quizzical look. "Simple," Aly said. "My dad will be your dad because I'll ask him to! Come over tomorrow. I'll set it up." I was so proud of Aly's response. The essence of the movement; friends helping friends.. Aly immediately knew what to do and activated The Power of WHO: friends helping friends. The next day I met with Ilana and listened to her goals, dreams, and career aspirations. I had several contacts in L.A. who could help her and was able to set her up with five interviews within her field of dreams. I then activated my Inner Circle WHO by personally calling each one, sharing Ilana's story, asking for WHO else they may know that could help Ilana. Before the day's end, Ilana had eight more interviews set and over the next two weeks, Ilana got five job offers with two of the companies bidding on her until the end before she chose the one she fell in love with!

I was one of Ilana's allies. We knew each other through my daughter and through that connection I was able to activate my WHO to help Ilana find the job she had hoped and dreamed about.

_____

_____

_____

_____

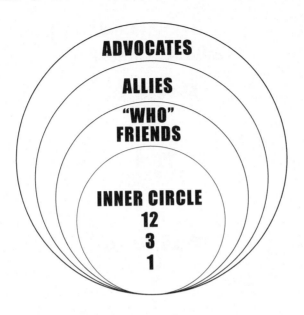

Advocates

"Advocates" can be people you know or, quite possibly, people you don't know. They may know of you through your business or some other affiliation, enough so to advocate on your behalf. The world is full of people who may be willing to advocate for you, which is why it is important to maintain a solid reputation and not burn bridges.

_____

_____

_____

_____

_____

_____

_____

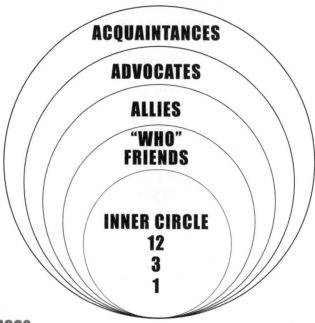

ACQUAINTANCES

ADVOCATES

ALLIES

"WHO"
FRIENDS

INNER CIRCLE
12
3
1

Acquaintances

"Acquaintances" are simply people we know who do not (yet) hold the title of friend. They are people we recognize, know at least their first name, and will greet with a smile or handshake and a few words of polite conversation. They can be co-workers, people who belong to a professional organization, fellow church-goers, service providers, etc.

Someone who is an acquaintance can quickly turn into to a friend but there is a price of admission. Use WHO discernment when talking with people. If you sense a genuine connection, it may be a clue that you should spend more time and develop a relationship with this person.

_____

_____

_____

_____

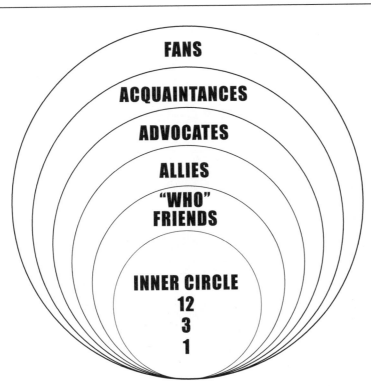

Fans

Fans are, well, fans. There may be people in this last sphere who don't know you, but know of you through your profession, philanthropic pursuits, volunteer work, published writings, public performances, or something of the like. Entertainment and sports personalities have fans, but you don't have to be on a national stage to draw a fan base. It's easy for your ego to get its feeding from fans, but healthy boundaries are necessary for a balanced life. This is a primary reason people who are in the public arena need to identify their WHO friends to know exactly who is a healthy relationship and who is not.

You now have a list of your own Inner Circle and have started writing the names of WHO friends from your past and present sphere of influence. You have also done a great deal of soul-searching as to who really is a friend and what is the price of admission to your life.

Now, it's time to Reach Out and Reconnect.

I've always heard that 80% of success was just showing up. But that has to be even truer with friendships! What good is it to have friends if you never talk to them? If you never send them a handwritten note, go to breakfast, lunch, dinner or an event? Who have you fallen out of contact with and need to Reconnect with? Don't forget that friends are different than acquaintances. Once someone has taken a place in your heart…they never leave! They are waiting for you to call-So Reach Out!

As you review these names, ask yourself these questions:

- Now that I've Reached Out, how can I be a better friend to these key people in my life?
- In what ways can I help them achieve their goals and dreams?
- What do I need to do to really connect?
- Have I declared my friendship?
- Do I remember birthdays, anniversaries?
- Do I ask about their grandparents, parents, and family?
- Do I talk about me or ask how they are doing? And really mean it?
- Have I bought them a gift, book, helped their kids, given them a reference, endorsement or a testimonial?

John Maxwell said it best: "People do not care how much you know until they know how much you care."

Reconnecting is real!

What specific ways can you Reconnect?

True friends empower you to find your purpose, define your objectives, reach for your dreams, fulfill your ambitions and achieve your goals!

So let's do a quick test to see how well we are communicating with the closest friends/family we have. We will just review our Inner circle friends. Record your friend's name, and then mark a check in the box below on how you specifically communicated with your "12" this past week? This is only a review sheet for you, so be real with your response.

Inner Circle Communication Chart

INNER CIRCLE NAME	TEXT	EMAIL	CALL	PERSONAL NOTE	FACEBOOK MESSAGE	BREAKFAST	LUNCH	DINNER	EVENT

CHAPTER 5

DARE TO DREAM

"I believe in destiny, and when destiny calls you must obey."
~Winston Churchill

Over the last 30 plus years in executive recruiting, I've had the opportunity to interview many great people, including presidents, generals, TV/studio executives, entrepreneurs, small business owners, university presidents, head coaches and others from all sorts of walks in life. Interestingly, I found two common links to all their stories of success. The first was that each had a particular story about "one person" that crossed their path and inspired them to "dare to dream." It was a short, but meaningful, conversation that changed the entire trajectory of their lives. The second common link was that each felt a "calling" that was unique to them and distinctive to their gifts and talents. In each case, they were drawn to it by some pre-wired, internal radar that acted upon them like a homing signal. Following that signal changed everything!

Is it possible for you to once again "dare to dream" and follow that signal you've been receiving all your life?

"Who are you? Who-who? Who-who?"

This question, made famous by the rock group by the same name, is more than just quizzical prose to ponder—it may be the single most important question you will answer to determine your destiny's course.

In this chapter, you'll learn that you are a uniquely created individual with a destiny to live a fulfilled, purposeful life. I will dare you to dream—and dream BIG—for the future that's still ahead of you. Whether you are 25 or 55, together we'll discover who you really are, what you want, and what really matters in order to achieve your life's purpose.

 In order to know what we want and determine what really matters, we must understand WHO we are and believe we have our own destiny.

What do you want to be when you grow up? When we were five, we had a quick answer to this question. However, we possibly heard it differently than how it's written: "Who do you want to be when you grow up?" or "What do you want to do when you grow up?" The internalization of how we hear this question, one that is a repeated theme throughout our childhood and adolescence, begins a two-pronged cycle of thinking that to some degree teaches us that our life's work is about emulating others within a lifestyle of doing.

Sounds rather mechanical, doesn't it? Emulating others is not necessarily bad, and "doing" is not bad at all, but contained within both trains of thought are subtleties that program us to perform and squelch our ability to dream. We've become human "doings" instead of human beings. And it's "being" that's great! "Being" allows us to dream again and the things we do that flow then from our dreams are more fulfilling, productive, and joyful.

Have you forgotten your dreams? When was the last time you dreamed? Is it possible that you once dreamed of living a different life from the one you're living now but just can't remember—something for which you're uniquely and wonderfully "wired?" Many of us have gotten sidetracked and forgotten our original dream, spending our lives doing derivative work. This memory lapse has become an epidemic. We have less and less time to calmly think about the direction our lives have taken and reflect on our current course. Did you give up on your dream? That would be a "Big Mistake!"

HOW YOUR PAST SPEAKS IN YOUR PRESENT AND FUTURE

Did you grow up in a household where your parent or parents enjoyed life? In what ways?

_____

_____

_____

_____

Did they enjoy their work (paid or unpaid)?

_____

What was your view of work when you were growing up?

_____

_____

_____

How was volunteering (for charitable) organizations, including church, viewed in your home?

_____

_____

Whom did you admire? Who do you know that finished (life) well? What was it about them you respected?

_____

_____

_____

What are some positive aspects from your formative years that you can apply to your life today?

_____

_____

_____

69% of the country believes that "a bad day at the beach is better than a good day at work"

We are purposed to work AND to enjoy our work. Somewhere along the way, however, we bought into the lie that our work, whether paid or volunteer, whether salaried executive or stay-at-home mom, is a part of life we muddle through and are not to enjoy. This is negative thinking and a primary reason our nation is built upon an empire of pharmaceuticals. Stress-related illness and disease kills millions each year. According to a 20 year study by Kaiser Permanente, 70% to 85% of all illnesses sending patients to their doctors were caused by stress. Not just aggravated by stress, but CAUSED by stress. It doesn't have to be this way.

Discovering who you are, *determining* what you want and *deciding* what matters most takes patience and a persistent and perpetual perseverance to press on as you overcome your fears. Stepping into the unknown can be intimidating, but it can also be exhilarating. They key is to not allow your exhilaration to turn to anxiety.

What specific fears do you think might be keeping you from enjoying a fulfilled life?

_____

_____

_____

There's a common reason many of us only use a small percentage of our gifts and talents. We're just too concerned about making mistakes! Even though we know "practice makes perfect," we feel the pressure to be perfect faster! We also place so much importance on the approval of others that we tend to get cautious and not take chances that would let us stand out in the crowd. And then worst of all, we accept someone else's standard of excellence and let it replace our own standard of doing our best. That's where friends make such a difference in our lives. They don't need you to be anybody other than who you already are. But, at the same time, they're glad to see you become something more. Once you're aware of your dream, these friendships will act like a kind of chisel that helps you carve away everything that doesn't look like you and your dream.

"Busyness" masquerades as effectiveness.

Busyness is another dream-robber that we need to unpack and examine before continuing on the journey. Busyness masquerades as effectiveness A busy life is typically not a productive or satisfying life. The law of sowing and reaping cannot be circumvented. What we sow deeply, we reap deeply. The problem is that many of us are stretched so thinly with our busy lives that our shallow sowing is not producing a healthy or bountiful harvest.

When asked to rank the elements of life that cause them the most stress, respondents placed "excessive noise in the environment" right behind "working/raising family."—National Stress Survey, Prevention Magazine

WHAT YOU LOVE

Discovering your dream will require you to find what you love. However, one of the great disconnects of life, a truly monumental error that people commonly make, is not allowing love to direct their course. Why? Because they don't know their own hearts, so they distrust themselves and their natural instincts.

When you allow yourself to be so programmed by the culture you're in that you become disconnected from your own heart, you render yourself unable to make decisions about what's best for your life and the lives of those you love. The real danger here is that you'll begin to follow somebody else's idea of fulfillment and success. You forget WHO and WHAT you are. You attempt to become someone or something else for which you are ill-suited.

In *The Power of WHO*, I listed several possible reasons why we get stuck doing what we don't want to do:

1. We Want to Be Somebody Else.

A person may admire someone for their achievements in life and want to be like them. But if that person doesn't possess the same skills, talents or gifts as that person, they will certainly fail. We fantasize about being someone we're not instead of realizing we've each been designed with a unique set of gifts, talents and skills.

Is there someone in your life you admire? What it is about them that you admire?

_____

_____

_____

2. Preoccupation!

We forget our dreams, and live unfulfilled lives, because we're preoccupied with time-wasting activities that do not matter to our overall purpose. I urge you to say no to a vegetative lifestyle. Turn off the TV, put down your iPad, close the laptop, power off your smartphone, and get to work fulfilling your purpose.

What do you do to "escape?"

_____

_____

_____

3. Living Someone Else's Dream for You

You may have allowed a parent, teacher, preacher, or some other authority figure to manufacture what they thought was a good identity for you. All of us need wise counselors and good guidance, but only from those who have no other agenda except to help us discover and develop what we love and are well-suited for.

How do you feel you might be living someone else's desire for your life? Explain.

_____

_____

_____

_____

> *I got a call from a friend who told me he had been let go from his company after 15 years. He was shocked! I said to him, "Congratulations! This is the greatest day of your life!" He said: "What?" I reminded him, "You hated that job! You got divorced in that job! You forgot "Who You Were" in that job! Isn't it time to do what you love?"*

STATUS QUO NO MORE

The status quo may seem safe, but it is robbing you from your life's purpose or that one thing you were meant to do. It is high time you redesigned your life to live it the way you've always wanted rather than living an obligated life.

A Simple Formula for Right Living

☐ Doing what you love

☐ With those you love

☐ In a place you/your spouse/family loves

 The core of true success is love.

What do you love?

_____

_____

I was in my twenties when I first joined my dad's executive search firm, Eastman & Beaudine. I never really thought about this being the job; I was seeking a field where I felt I could excel and where I like the people I worked with and they liked me. I became very successful, but after several years of doing the same thing, I began a growing uneasiness and a longing for something more. I liked executive search, but I loved sports. I often wondered if there was a way to involve my passion for sports with my career as an executive recruiter.

One day, I approached my dad with the frustrations I was feeling. He asked me two very simple, yet direct, questions: "What do you want to do? What do you love?"

Those questions awakened my dream. And, in a flash, I began to speak with clarity about how I would like to develop a division of our firm that would accommodate the entertainment and sports industries.

His response, "Go get it!"

POWER IN THE PRESENT

If there is hope in the future, there is power in the present. This principle is vital. The most satisfied people are those that live in the NOW.

Four ways you can remain laser-focused on the present:

1. Let go of the past. Dwelling on the past only clouds your future and ruins your today.
2. Do today what needs to be done today. Don't neglect your current responsibilities.
3. Know, prioritize, and pursue your primary goals. Don't pursue goals that no longer make sense.
4. Try making a "Not To Do List".

Of the four ways listed, which one do you feel you need to work on the most?

_____

_____

_____

What steps can you take today to make a change?

_____

_____

Contrary to what you may have been taught, life cannot be lived in compartments. Your life's priorities are like a tiered fountain where each area spills into the others and affects everyone around you.

Knowing and living your priorities today will make a significant impact on tomorrow's dreams, goals, and relationships.

One of my heroes is Zig Ziglar! When he speaks with large groups, he always asks two great questions. The first: "Is there one decision you could make today that would make tomorrow worse?" With that question he always gets a resounding "yes" from the crowd. Then he asks the second question: "What one thing can you do, or one decision can you make, that will make tomorrow better?" And then the crowd goes silent. It's amazing to consider how powerful our choices really are and how they can affect not only our lives but the lives of those we love.

So let me ask you what Zig asked the crowd: What one thing can you do, or one decision can you make, that would make your relationship with (name) better?

_____

_____

From years of experience, I can tell you with certainty that making your dreams a reality requires assistance. Unfortunately, most people never get out of life what they want because they:

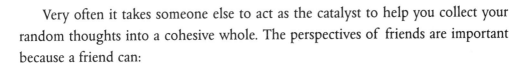

- Do not know WHO to ask for help

- Ask the wrong WHO for help

- Ask vague questions

Very often it takes someone else to act as the catalyst to help you collect your random thoughts into a cohesive whole. The perspectives of friends are important because a friend can:

- Ask good questions and think through processes (brainstorm)

- See things about yourself that you have failed to see

- Encourage you (or give permission) for you to pursue your dreams and goals

These people are closer than you think.

LISTEN TO MARY'S STORY

What once was lost now is found!

I was once forced to take a Dale Carnegie course. My supervisor thought the course would help me be a better manager and basically ordered me to sign up. The course lasted for 12 weeks and was all about teaching you how to strengthen your interpersonal relationships, handle stress, and adapt to a fast-changing workplace. Learning how to speak in public is a significant portion of the course.

I initially thought the course was a joke—until I heard Mary's story. Mary was an "orphan" whose husband had recently left her for another woman. Her accounting firm had transferred her to a new city where she didn't know anyone. She appeared shy, sad, and hurt, which were all major hindrances to being a good public speaker. During the third week of class, we had to give an impromptu speech on the subject of pets. This was Mary's chance to improve on her earlier performances where she'd completely bombed.

Given the subject of pets, Mary became energized, passionate and joyful as she talked about her boxer, Lucille. I was asked to provide Mary with direct feedback about her speech with three positive things I had received from her. I began by telling her, "Great job, Mary! You really know a lot about dogs! As you gave your speech, you clearly had everyone's attention. I have to tell you, Mary, if I were you, I wouldn't be an accountant any longer. You've convinced me, and I think everyone else in the room, that you should be a veterinarian. I'm sure I'm not the first to say this to you, but I believe this is your calling."

Mary seemed different after that night. She became more and more confident and each week became more and more vocal at encouraging others in class. The night of Mary's speech was a turning point for all of us. The rest of the course sailed by. On graduation night, Mary addressed the class this way, "When I began this course I was a shy, unhappy divorcee with no friends, family, or hope. Today, I stand here a changed woman. I hope you all don't feel uncomfortable when I tell you that you saved my life!" She then gave each of us personalized letters, but asked to read the one to me aloud.

In the letter she said that what I shared that night of her speech about her "calling" reawakened a dream she'd had since she was nine years old to become a veterinarian. She announced to the class that just yesterday, she got a job as a veterinarian's assistant and they were going to pay for her to go back to school to fulfill her dream of becoming a veterinarian.

You see, Mary like a lot of people had forgotten her dream. A few catalysts triggered her dream to remember what she had always loved. With the encouragement of others, she discovered WHO she really is, WHAT really mattered most in her life, and WHAT she truly wanted. Mary is now walking on a happier, healthier path to living her destiny.

"Living the life you love has the almost magical quality of keeping you young, vibrant and healthy."

Growing up, what was your dream? What goals did you wish to attain? What did you hope to become? Is that dream still alive in you? Is it realistic? If not, can it be transformed into a new dream that is more appropriate for who and where you are today?

_____

_____

_____

_____

_____

_____

What steps need to be taken to realize your dream? Further education or training?

_____

_____

_____

_____

Can you fulfill your dream where you are currently living, or do you need to relocate?

_____

Discovering what makes you feel fulfilled, satisfied and content is a significant part of connecting WHAT matters most to WHO you are to WHAT you want.

> **"Each of us has an assignment, a purpose, a dream all our own that we need to discover or rediscover."**

Do you know WHAT matters most in your life? Don't let a sudden illness or a tragedy define your priorities. The best way to determine what matters most in your life is for you to take time to reflect, listen, and plan. We all must rediscover the lost discipline of practicing solitude by setting aside (scheduling) regular time daily to clear your thoughts. All great leaders throughout history have added this great discipline.

The operative word here is "practice." Practicing solitude at the start is tough. It requires patience and giving yourself permission to not be very good at it at first. But more than patience, it requires action. You need to do it. Permission granted!

How to Practice Solitude

- Unplug from technology
- Go away from your house to a place where you can think (away from noise)
- Read inspirational writings or quotes
- Pray / Meditate / Quiet your soul
- Take a long walk by yourself
- Breathe in fresh air of renewal
- Enjoy the simple beauty and sounds of nature

You probably feel calmer just reading through that list, but you must carve out the time to do it, and then do it again and again until you've made a discipline out of your decision to practice solitude.

The other day I was traveling on business and was trying to write but wasn't feeling any inspiration. The plane was loud so I grabbed my iPod to listen to some soothing music. I closed my eyes and tried to just let my mind go. I was really enjoying myself and dozed off when all of a sudden—BAM! The flight attendant hit my leg with the cart going by! Oh my gosh, I winced in pain and she ran to the front of the plane to get something. She came back apologizing and was so nice. She wanted to give me a free drink or some food tickets. I told her it wasn't necessary since I was probably at fault with my leg sticking out. When she came back by later I gave her a signed copy of *The Power of WHO*. I told her I appreciated her kindness. She asked what the book was about and I gave her a quick summary. Then she started crying all of a sudden. She told me that for the last two years she had been writing a book but had recently quit. She had lost her inspiration. This 5 minute conversation was overwhelming to her. She told me that she wanted to go back to the front of the plane to start reading the book right then. After a little while she came back and said: "Did you write this book for me?" I laughed. Then she got serious and asked me: "Do you think it's possible that my hitting your leg was not just by chance, but an opportunity for you to get me back on track for my dream?" "Yes!" I said. "As crazy as that may sound—I wouldn't doubt it!" Over the next hour of the trip, this question kept bubbling up inside me: "What if I hadn't taken time-out for solitude? Gotten quiet?" We probably never would have met!

Make "Solitude" a priority in your life. Remind yourself to open your calendar and schedule some time. Make it as much of a priority as your most important client meeting or your child's birthday celebration. Everyone else will be glad you did!

Make "Solitude" a priority in your life.

CHAPTER 6

ALL YOU NEED IS 1/10,000!

"Bob Beaudine has figured out what makes the world turn!
The Power of WHO **is without question the answer we've**
been searching for on why and how to be successful!"
~June Jones, Head Football Coach SMU

Early in my career, I became aware that the world operates within a framework of laws and principles. It doesn't take long to see that there's a clear correlation between the understanding and use of these principles and the results achieved. When it comes to connecting with your dreams and goals, the golden rule is WHO always comes before WHAT. Both are essential, but the choice of where to start is of paramount importance. Starting with WHO rather than WHAT will send you in the right direction and, more importantly, will keep you focused on what's truly essential.

In this chapter, I'll show you several examples of how these laws and principles of WHO can be applied across your life. I'm not talking about a promotion here. I'm talking about a seismic shift that would change the entire trajectory of your life. Is it writing a book, learning to fly, losing thirty pounds and getting into shape? Is it starting your own company, or devoting your full energies to your passion? It could be in sports, music, the arts, charity, or politics. This WHO strategy is the treasure map you've been seeking. It will help you better understand how the world turns. How just 1 friend and their concentric circles of influence—makes all the difference.

THE AGENT

When I first started seeking out a literary agent for *The Power of WHO*, the long list of agents throughout the country to consider was I have to say… rather confusing.

Also since this was my first book, people told me that getting anyone to actually read the manuscript would be a monumental task, especially a top literary agent. Well, I saw this as the perfect opportunity to use The Power of WHO and my "100/40 Strategy." Why? Because I believe: "You Already Know Everyone You Need To Know!" And if this didn't work for me here—then it wouldn't work for you. But it did for me and it will for you!

I started out doing some research. In real estate, we've been told it's about location, location, location. In "100/40 Strategy" it's about preparation, preparation, preparation. So before I asked my WHO for help, I needed to know who were the top agents in the country that handled books like mine. I went to Barnes and Noble that afternoon and looked up some top New York Times Bestselling authors in the inspiration/business section to see if possibly I could get lucky and these writers mentioned their agents in their acknowledgments. Score! One name clearly shined out above the rest—Jan Miller. I was amazed when I read she lived in Dallas. Instead of being intimidated and going for lesser known agents, Jan was my goal! I actually wrote her name on my office chalk board so I could see it. JAN MILLER. From what I had read, she handled Tony Robbins, Steven Covey, Dr. Phil, Joel Osteen, and TD Jakes, just to name a few. I thought Bob Beaudine needs to be on that list!

So my next step was to send an email to a portion of my "100 list" saying;

"Hi _____, As you know, I have just finished writing *The Power of WHO* and I'm looking for a top literary agent to represent me. I need your help! Do you by chance know the name Jan Miller?"

In just ten minutes, I got five emails saying they were friends with Jan! Are you kidding? All five wanted to assist me in any way they could with letters, email recommendations or personal calls to Jan on my behalf. I was shocked! None of these five are in the publishing industry, but somehow over the years they were friends of friends of hers. My follow-up email to each was: "'WHO' knows Jan the best?" I knew I needed to put my best foot forward if I was going to get a shot at being one of her clients.

You won't believe this but one of the five was almost like family to Jan and her husband! He actually worked with Jan's husband when he first moved to Dallas. So, I went to lunch with (my friend) Keenan Delaney and asked for his support. To my surprise he had already had dinner with Jan and had tee'd up a twenty minute meeting for me with Jan Miller! Twenty minutes turned into one of the best two hour meetings I've ever been in! A literal *WHO*-fest that ended by Jan signing me on the spot! It was magic from the start. Not only had Jan read the book because of her friend's recommendation, but she loved the concept and was telling me Power of WHO stories of her own.

You have a **WHO network**, a "community of friends" that's been built up over many years with love and unconditional giving. This particular network of friends, if asked, will actually come to your aid. But you must ask: WHO are these amazing gifts in your life? Jot down their names again here and "declare" them.

WHO networking isn't about introducing yourself into opportunities—it's about having the power of favor and being introduced the right way! Whether it's a date, a job interview, or making a big sales pitch, having great references, endorsements and testimonials are your most powerful allies. When your WHO says you're great, you are! Which friends of yours introduce you well? Write them here. WHO got you jobs in the past? Write their names down. WHO introduced you to your mate, has given you a loan—They should be in your "WHO Hall of Fame!"

Don't make the mistake of thinking you don't already know enough people who can help you on your quest. You need to understand that your WHAT will never come into play until your WHO brings you across. Write down which friends have opened doors, helped you across bridges, and gotten you big deals…Just Because! Don't forget to include what they did for you. It's a great exercise to reflect on these times.

_____   _____

_____   _____

_____   _____

_____   _____

_____   _____

_____   _____

_____   _____

_____   _____

_____   _____

When you consider that each of the people in your circle of friends has great influence with *their* circle of friends, you can begin to grasp the true Power of WHO! Imagine if you had a close friend who knew just the right person, who already works in the company of your dreams and would open the door for you? Now that would rock! I've got news for you – you do! It happens every day.

Let's stop for a second and do some math. If you have a 100 friends and I have 100 friends, how many do we have together? 200? No! It's actually more than that. It's 10,000! How can that be? Because your friends have other friends—think of it as "WHO Squared!" But, the real question is: do we really need 100 friends? Because a 100 friends x 100=10,000! That's a lot of people! Can we deal with that many people? I don't think so! And to be honest, you and I don't have 100 true friends anyway.

So... what if you had 50 friends and I had 50? Well, we would have 2,500 friends between us. That's still too big! Can we deal with that many? No, not really! That's why just having 12 friends, 3 close and 1 best friend is so effective and hopeful.

GOLF PRO

I have an old friend named Will Brewer who used to be the director of golf at my country club. When he moved to Nashville, we had to be extra creative in order to see each other. So, we would try to play in a golf tournament together each year. One year, in Colorado, I learned a great lesson about a "hidden dynamic" within The Power of WHO.

At the end of each round of golf, Will and I would sit around with the other foursomes and talk. Will would always go out of his way to introduce me to others saying; "Have you met my close friend Bob Beaudine? He's the best executive recruiter in the country." You've got to love guys like Will!

It was interesting; when he introduced me to people he didn't know well (acquaintances) they usually said: "Great to meet you Bob" and that was it. But when he introduced me to someone he knew well, (his WHO) the introduction and endorsement was so much more significant to that man because of the trust he had in Will, a trust developed over many years.

One day one of Will's WHO friends turned to me and asked, "Bob, do you handle executive searches for CFOs?" I said, "Absolutely." He said, "Great, call me next Tuesday." It caught me off guard. I thought, "Huh? That's it?" Just Will saying I was great to one of his close friends and I land a big executive search from a major company! Is that possible?

That one incident blew my paradigm on networking. I really never thought that my golf pro friend would turn out to be a major asset to my executive recruiting business. The idea had simply never crossed my mind. I had so compartmentalized my approach to networking that this was a real eye-opener. I'm not sure I realized until that moment that my "12-3-1" and "100 list" friends were quite different from all of my business acquaintances who had been acquired through years of traditional networking.

My WHO friends, on the other hand, could and would help me any chance they got, and I could help them. Yes, you have to be competent in your field, but you and I both know that doing our jobs isn't the tough part. Many times, it's just getting the opportunity to perform that's hard today.

Is it possible that someone you already know, someone who likes you, can actually help you? One great friend out of the 10,000 in your WHO world. Who are those in your life? Has there been one friend that acts like Will in your life?

_____

How do you stay in touch with your old friends that live out of town?

_____

_____

_____

_____

_____

Today, you and I need the special relationships we've been given in our lives to not only survive but to thrive! So WHO will you turn to today and WHAT will you ask them to do?

_____

_____

A TV host asked me recently: "What if your friends are all losers?" I groaned and said to the host: "Come on Lisa, there's something great in everyone! We've just made the mistake of looking at our family and friends one-dimensionally. They've got friends too, you know! I asked her if she had ever seen that Verizon commercial on TV with the guy who is standing out in front all those people. That's what I mean when I say: "You Got WHO!" It's your community, your WHO. Jane Howard said it best: "Call it a clan, call it a network, call it a tribe, call it a family. Whatever you call it, whoever you are, you need one!"

THE CRISIS

After a recent speech, a woman came up to meet me and just hugged me. She didn't seem to want to let go! Over the last two years speaking around the country, I've found this message of The Power of WHO can have that kind of effect on people because it's so inspirational, so hopeful.

She said her name was Cindy and was sorry she didn't bring any money to buy a book. I signed one for her one anyway because she was so nice! I had no idea she was a former breast cancer survivor when we talked. Her attitude was so bright, so uplifting to everyone around her. But, as I learned from her later, after a normal check-up with her doctor, she got a very discouraging report that the cancer had returned and this time was stage four.

She told me that after reading *The Power of WHO* she felt different, stronger, somehow better prepared for news like this. She wasn't going to take the same tact she had in previous years by looking for help from people she didn't know. This time, she immediately reached out to family who lived in Houston and asked them if they had any contacts that could get her into MD Anderson, which has one of the top experimental testing programs in the world for this type of cancer. It only took a week or so before, through her sister and brother-in law's community of friends, Cindy was walking down the halls of MD Anderson!

But like all journeys, there are twists and turns. And how we handle these are crucial. The doctor at MD Anderson that she was introduced to was great but not the right person. He led her to one experimental testing program which led to another and another. All along the way, Cindy stayed positive and befriended everyone she met. This is extremely hard to do in a crisis. The shock and energy drain can be overwhelming. You must have a support group in times like these, a faith in something bigger. Cindy had that! She stayed focused on the solution rather than the problem. One of the people she met along the way was an assistant to an important doctor in the field of study she needed. This friendship with her turned out to be the catalyst.

It's interesting to look back and see how the patterns woven into the fabric of our circumstances have led us to where we are now. In Cindy's case it was an assistant, not a doctor, a person that most of us in a crisis wouldn't recognize; we just might pass her by. This young woman, however, was celebrated by Cindy during the process, not tolerated. She joined Cindy's WHO team, and when she heard of a unique experimental testing program that would be a perfect fit for Cindy, she opened the door for her and walked her through!

> **The one thing in life that gives radiance above other things is that there is something great just around the corner!**

Could we have all been missing it all these years?! Was our WHO in life supposed to assist us in every phase of our life . . . physical, mental, and spiritual? Were they meant to be our support team, our personal marketing and PR team, our financial advisers, our business and life coaches, our mentors, or our personal board of directors? Could they have helped us over the years with finding the right doctor, lawyer, nursing home, special tickets—you name it? YES!!

At the first sign of trouble, call a friend! All it takes is one great WHO friend to share some compassion, encouragement, direction and insight that will help you get you back on track. But this will only happen if you're humble and wise enough to ask, listen, and then let those who are near to you–Help You.

Cindy was wise! Make sure you don't superimpose an old agenda onto a whole new set of circumstances. It never works. It's time for a New Plan! Because, if you want something you've never had, you're going to have to do some things you've never done!

Review your fears and concerns with those you love! A WHO friend will intercept you on the dark path you've taken and redirect your steps back on to the path of light. They know you, care for you, and will remind you that you have a future and a hope.

The great philosopher, Mike Tyson once said: "Everyone has a plan until they're Hit!" Maybe he's smarter than we think! Because a "Knock Down" can take us all into unfamiliar territory. It can disorient you unless you stay alert and immediately acclimate to your new circumstances. When you're hit, don't dwell on the past. Order yourself, "Eyes forward!" There's a rock-solid rule about being Knocked Down that will help you tremendously. Write this rule down and keep it where you'll see it every day until it becomes a part of you, for it will be a very powerful ally.

Embrace the unknown as friendly and ultimately beneficial.

In a crisis, WHO do you turn to? Friends or Acquaintances?

Cast away all those fears. Stay positive like Cindy. Befriend everyone! You never know where that help will come from—you just have to have faith that it IS coming!

When I get Knocked Down in life, I ask myself these three simple questions.

1. Does God know my situation? (Yes, He's God.)

2. Is He ok with the situation/problem I'm in? (He must be-I'm in it!)

3. Does He have a Great Plan/Purpose ahead for me and you?
   (Yes! Absolutely! And then I start looking for it!)

TIMESHARE

I have a friend in Mexico who sells timeshares. Through my association with him, I discovered that the top 3% of timeshare sales reps operate according to The Power of WHO. The other 97% somehow go a different direction.

The primary goal of every timeshare rep during their first few years in the business is to build a base of one hundred clients. It's hard work and long hours but, if done correctly it can pay off big time! What's interesting, however, is that the 3% of the sales reps, the top 3%, have an entirely different strategy of success than everybody else. Why? Let's look closer.

Once the top 3% hit their mark of 100 clients, they choose to go deeper with these relationships rather than wider. They give them the royal treatment. How? They're nurtured, cultivated, and pampered with great customer service. They don't compartmentalize them into a sector called business, but instead see them as "friends." They spend a lot of time thanking them and are always on the alert for whatever extra they can do.. Their three word mantra is:

"Yes, I can!"

They help them with hotel arrangements, cars, restaurants, babysitters, and a better location on the property—whatever. They help with ideas on weddings, birthday parties, and anniversaries—nothing is too much to ask. They think of their clients as "gifts" in their lives, and it shows.

Why would these 3% do all this "extra work" on clients they've already sold? Shouldn't they be out like the other 97% of the reps trying to find their next 100 prospects? What's up? They discovered a secret called "The Law of Less." It's actually very simple. Their strategy is to "dance with the one that brung ya!" They believe they "Already Know Everyone They Need To Know" for their present and future success. These "Special 100" clients, if shown extra care and attention, will be their golden egg, their oil well, or their IPO in the coming years.

What these top 3% have learned is that you focus single-mindedly on the ones you have in hand. There's a hidden benefit: they will start to work for you! How? They will:

- Buy one more week on the property because they feel so good.
- Upgrade from a one bedroom to a two or three bedroom unit over time.
- Introduce their WHO friends who will also buy a timeshare.
- Tell the sales manager that they have "the greatest sales rep in the world and he's the top reason they are there!"

What does this all mean? It means more sales, happier customers, and a more enjoyable lifestyle!

Wouldn't life be a little better if we "did life with friends?" I mean actually treated all our clients like friends. Wouldn't your business be better? What are a few things you can do tomorrow morning to begin treating somebody you work with, or one of your clients or customers, as a friend?

_____

_____

_____

In this story, the top 3% timeshare sales reps "Got it!" But how did the other 97% miss it? Where are you with your thinking? Have you bought into the concept that business and friends are taboo? Do you ever barbeque on weekends with your clients, clubs, associations, church, etc.? Or… "Are you seeking something else and missing something more?"

The top 3% timeshare reps don't make that mistake. They treasure what they've been given and also expect to meet new people that they "click" with from time to time. When they do, they don't let them get away, because they know a rare gem when they see it.

There are unchanging laws and principles that govern the natural world. And sometimes it just takes a simple question to begin the flow that brings all those tributaries of thought into a common stream. Sometimes, it takes someone who sees something in you that you can't see in yourself and is able to speak it to you in a way that enables you to see it, too. Sometimes someone gives you permission to do what you've always wanted to do.

Anyone on a great quest is looking for clues that will help guide them. So make sure when it comes to connecting with your dreams and goals you don't

"Sometimes the questions are complicated and the answers are simple."
~Dr. Seuss

miss your cues because the golden rule is WHO always comes before WHAT. Both are essential, but the choice of where to start is of paramount importance. Starting with WHO rather than WHAT will send you in the right direction and, more importantly, will keep you focused on what's truly essential.

CHAPTER 7

DETOURS, PITFALLS, UNEXPECTED TWISTS AND HEARTACHE

"Every problem has a gift for you in its hands."

~ Richard Bach

It's almost a proverb. People get pumped up about their dreams and goals and begin moving in that direction but encounter a few bumps along the way. The person gives up, just before something great was about to happen. Even though they desperately want to succeed, they allow themselves to become discouraged, and then make the one fatal mistake that totally kills their momentum—they quit. Don't let that be you! Big Mistake!

Paul Harvey once said: "In times like these it helps to recall that there have always been times like these." Have you been here? Are you here now? Well, don't be discouraged—what appears to be a dead end…might only be a detour!

I want to share four simple truths to help you re-focus when you've lost your momentum or way due to circumstances beyond your control. It's never time to stop believing in yourself, in your dreams, and in better days just around the corner.

Secret #1 — Don't Ever Forget Who You Are!

I'll never forget…My dad taking me backstage to see Frank Sinatra after one of his shows in Las Vegas. I was about 13 at the time but the moment made an indelible imprint on my approach to business and life. You see, Frank Sinatra was also known as the Chairman of the Board and no one else was like him at the time. So the idea of going backstage and actually meeting him, having a moment with Mr. Sinatra was not only improbable but was something most normal people would find extremely intimidating to even try.

But dad always taught me that…"nothing can hold back or deter the firm resolve of a determined soul." When we got to the backstage door there was a very large man guarding the entrance. My dad announced that we were here to see Frank Sinatra. The guard snickered without really looking at us and said he wasn't available. It was then I heard my dad forcefully and confidently say: "Tell-em Frank Beaudine from Chicago is here." "I'm sorry" the guard said now looking at us, "He's not available!" "Listen," my dad said with a stern face. "My son and I don't have a lot of time! Tell-em Frank Beaudine—from Chicago!"

> **nothing can hold back or deter the firm resolve of a determined soul**

Now the guard had to think quickly… What if we did know Mr. Sinatra? Would he be upset with him that he didn't bring his friend Frank Beaudine and his son back to say hello? The reality was that we didn't know Mr. Sinatra at all, didn't say we did, but the guard didn't know that! So, it came down to confidence, boldness and one of the "classic lines" I've ever heard—"Tell-em Frank Beaudine from Chicago." What happened next was amazing. The guard said, "Hold on" and went back to tell Mr. Sinatra we were outside. It was only 30 seconds before we were ushered in. What did Mr. Sinatra say when we entered? "Frank!! How are you? How's Chicago my friend?"

So, the first secret is simple: Know WHO you are!" Act like it! Walk in that confidence. The Frank Sinatras of the world want to meet you! Be prepared, confident, bold, and brave!

What's hindered you from taking on a new challenge at work?

_____

_____

At home or in your community?

_____

_____

Life's made up of "Moments and Choices." Don't miss yours! Be a Moment Maker today! It's WHO you are!!

Secret #2   Do What You REALLY Love To Do

There's this philosophy out there today that the more "general" you are in your approach to whatever you are seeking, the better chance you'll have at getting "it." As a CEO of an executive search firm, that's confusing to me and I'm telling you it's not true. In fact, the truth is just the opposite. You are most likely to reach your goals and realize your dreams if you know exactly what you want, why you want it and what are the specific gifts and talents you bring that make you "special," makes you "stand out" from others. The one and only Zig Ziglar said: **"Only the inspired in life-Inspire! Inspiration fuels passion, and passion wins the job, the campaign, and pretty much everything else!"**

But one of life's great paradoxes is that by not deciding, by just sitting there up on that fence waiting, you're actually making a decision. You're actually pulling yourself out of the game! If you don't decide WHO and WHAT you want to be or if you're not willing to pay the price to get there, then somebody else will handle those things for you. Does that sound like a threat? Now, I don't know about you, but I don't want somebody else's plan for my life! There's got to be a better way! There is!

The important life principle here is simple: "Let WHAT you want be an extension of WHO you are."

When you discover *WHAT* you want, this great thing will happen: *WHO* you are becomes clearer because WHAT you truly want will derive from WHO you really are. In other words, it will tap into your personality, your skill set, your passion. It will fit you like a glove. If it doesn't, you're missing the mark. And I don't want you to miss it. Because if you do, you'll run the risk of joining the ranks of all the unhappy people in the world who are stuck in a rut and dissatisfied with their lives.

I was asked by a good friend, Lisa LeMaster (one of the top crisis/communications consultants in the country) to speak at her daughter Elissa's public relations class at the SMU Cox School of Business. What a great night! I told the class after my talk, if they wanted me to sign their book and talk for a minute or so about their dream, I would be waiting in the back. I wasn't actually shocked when 90% of the class got in line and waited patiently for their moment to talk. Why? Because everybody has a dream and needs to declare it. The Power of WHO message is on this generation's heart! They want to follow their path, their calling, and don't want to go to cubicle #3 never to be seen or heard. They don't want just "a job," even if it pays well, but isn't more fulfilling that the jobs most of their parents have. Their worst fear is ending up looking like the guy in cubicle #6 with his stapler!

No! They want to do a job they love, with people they love in a place they love, where their family loves to live and they can do it for the right reasons! So, after class I asked each student just two questions: **"What's Your Dream Job?"** and **"What Do You Love To Do?"**

At first, they dodged my questions, saying "Oh, Mr. Beaudine, I don't know." I said, "Sure you do! It's ok, you can tell me!" Then they threw out something lame, hoping no one behind them in the line would know their true desires. How embarrassing it would be if someone laughed or scoffed at their dream. But I wasn't budging. I didn't accept their vague answer, so the students got bolder and then said what was closer to their heart but not really the dream. This is where friends, family, mentors, coaches, and teachers can be a world of help. We can encourage those we love to not be afraid or embarrassed to declare their dreams. And once they do, we can build on it. That's what I told this class that evening. "You must dream out loud! Go ahead, let it loose," I encouraged them. And then, out of nowhere, from the deep inner part of their heart, each student boldly and confidently shared their dream! It was amazing! And when they did, I told each student, "Now you are ready to get started!"

You see, only with this new revelation, this voicing of the dream, can you create an action plan. Only then can you make the lists that you so desperately need. Lists that include your 12-3-1, the 100 *WHO* list (your support team) and the 40 *WHAT list* (the 40 specific people in each of those dream jobs/organizations you need to know to get that dream job). Only then can your family and friends begin to help.

Every organization welcomes the passionate worker with the right skill set and great attitude. But the only way you can have passion is to be inspired by something you love. So ask yourself, "What do I love?" Start digging. Start asking the tough questions! Go on that Wilderness Journey! Once you determine what you love, you'll have the clue you need to push you further along on the path toward connecting with your dream.

What are your recurring dreams? If you haven't thought about them in a while, let me remind you that you have a purpose and a set of dreams all your own that you need to discover or rediscover. These dreams are unique to you. Take a few minutes and write them down now. Be specific!

_____

_____

_____

_____

_____

_____

_____

Next, you need to declare them to your WHO friends. When we allow others access to our personal world, we give them the opportunity to see into us in ways we're not able to always see ourselves. You also need to help those closest to you to see the potential you see in *them* and allow others to give you clues about what they see in you. Write down WHO you are going to declare your dreams to this week.

_____

_____

What are you just naturally good at? You've always been good at it. It comes easy to you. What's your passion? Don't be fooled into pursuing just position, power, and money, or you'll miss out on the true treasures of peace, happiness, and deep-down contentment. These are the things that truly satisfy. It's not uncommon for people to overlook their unique gifts and talents simply because they don't see them as any big deal. But they are a Big Deal! Talk to your family and WHO friends! They have a perspective of your gifts and talents that you just might be unable to see. You have friends and friends of friends who will help you simply because they feel you're part of them, they are part of you, and you like each other— don't take this for granted. They can and will help you if you'll ask them! So ask! What are some of your gifts and talents you are most at peace and happy when applying them at work or with your WHO friends?

_____

_____

_____

_____

Secret #3 You Must Be Willing to Take A Risk

In my role as an executive recruiter, I had the opportunity of placing June Jones as SMU's head football coach. Getting him to leave Hawaii (paradise), where he was a legend, and was completing a season where he went 12-0 to move to Dallas to coach SMU who went 1-11 that year, was no small feat. It took a WHO team effort to accomplish. People never thought he would come, it never crossed their mind, and in fact why would we even try? Because…

. . . possible things aren't worth much, it's those crazy impossible things that keep us passionate and alive!

June Jones has a great story. As a quarterback in college he played for Oregon, Hawaii, and Portland State. His year at Portland State was epic and got him an opportunity to be in the NFL with the Atlanta Falcons. Unfortunately, he played behind Steve Bartkowski and two others. It looked bleak for him in his third season; he wasn't getting any opportunity to show what he could do.

In their last preseason game, with three minutes to go in the first half, the Falcons were trailing Green Bay 28-0. On the first play of a two minute drive, Steve Bartkowski dislocated his index finger when he hit his hand on a defensive tackle's helmet. All the coaches and players were looking down the field at his completed pass. No one was looking at Steve grimacing in pain as he came off the field. What happened next? Seeing the confusion and knowing they were in a two minute situation, June put on his helmet and ran into the game! Everyone was stunned. He put himself in!

The first play June called, he completed a 20-yard pass for a first down. As he looked to the sideline, head coach Leeman Bennett said nothing. The #2 and #3 quarterbacks had their helmets and each was ready to come in. After two more passes, June threw a touchdown! The Falcons onside kicked and on the last play of the half, June threw another touchdown pass to bring the Falcons to 28-14. As he and the team ran off, he thought to himself, "That was fun!"

In the locker room no one said anything to June. As he ran out to the field, he thought, "At least I had that opportunity." Then he was stunned when Coach Bennett called him over to start the second half. Even though Atlanta lost that preseason game 38-35, June threw for a Falcon record 386 yards and four touchdown passes! June Jones took a risk. Great people do that. They have an inner confidence, a panache that's not arrogance but alway faithful to their call. They believe as Winston Churchill said; **"When destiny calls you must answer!"** June did, so should you!

June Jones was looking for his opportunity. He sensed it. You and I need to develop the ability to cease the opportunities that life sets before us. Though we often miss the obvious, these once in a lifetime chances are easy to see if we train ourselves to keep our eyes, mind and heart open. Nike's great line: "Just Do It" seems sparse in its austere simplicity, but behind its profound wisdom is the stuff dreams are made of.

Think about a time you saw an opportunity. Did you take the risk? How did you feel with your choice? Would you make the same choice today?

_____

_____

_____

_____

_____

_____

Secret #4 Be Careful WHO is on your WHO List

I thought they were my WHO? What do you do when you get hurt?

I've been hurt deeply by someone I trusted, by someone I thought was my WHO friend. How about you? I let a couple people into my Inner Circle only to find out they weren't my WHO at all. It was a body and soul blow! I have to tell you it was a huge setback. I was caught off guard. How did I miss it? Did I wish qualities on them that they didn't have? Did we outgrow our friendship? Was it my fault? Here I am writing the book about doing life with WHO friends and still BAM, I get the hammer! But now, as time has gone by and I had some time to reflect with my family, friends, and mentors, I found out I'm not alone. In fact, it's happening all around me. It doesn't make me feel less hurt, but it clearly made me feel more grateful for the gifts of faithful WHO friendships I have been given.

Rejection is a severe teacher and you'll most likely log some time in this classroom at some point in your life. But rejection can be even more instructive than favor because it forces you to come to grips with "Who you really are" and "Who you're not." It lets you know "Where you don't belong" and "Who you don't belong with."

A prominent football coach called me after practice recently, "Bob I just read *The Power of WHO*, I had to call you; it was great!" I thanked him. He said, "The first time I read it, you inspired me! The second time I read it, I discovered you wrote many deep principles here, didn't you?" I said "Yes, it took me an extra year and a half." He said; "Well, the third time I read it, I colored coded it and tabbed it, reading it chapter by chapter with my wife." "You read my book three times?" I asked. He said, "Yes! The reason for my call was to tell you how impactful it was for us to actually write down and declare our 12-3-1. You must tell others to do that! When my wife and I showed each other our list of 12—I was shocked when my wife frowned at me and asked how 2 of my 12 names even got on my list! She felt they shouldn't even be in my 100—they weren't my WHO! I'll never forget you and your book for that, Bob!"

Some people come into your life for a reason or season and then...poof ... they're gone. Some you can get back, but others, it just won't happen. It even happened to Jesus! Has this happened to you? Are you more cautious now? Are you unwilling to let people into your Inner Circle? I can understand this, but I'm encouraging you not to allow bitterness to take root. There is a price of admission for friendship. Not just "Any WHO" makes your Inner Circle! Recognizing your true authentic WHO friends you can trust from the myriad of acquaintances that crowd around your life is difficult. And even with all best efforts, you will be treated unfairly and suffer undeserved hurt by a close friend. Back in 1850, it happened to Lord Alfred Tennyson. He wrote a poem about it. He wanted to make sure we didn't give up on WHO friends or love. I'm sure you know his great line by heart:

"Tis better to have loved and lost, than never to have loved at all."

Your pot of gold (whatever that represents to you) won't be found with people who don't like you. You'll never succeed with people who devalue you. They have no appreciation for your gifts and talents or the contribution you bring. Now would be a great time to reevaluate your associations and make some decisions about whom you're going to walk with into the future. Take a moment, reflect on WHO you need to spend more time with AND what kinds of things you can do together.

_____

_____

_____

_____

_____

_____

_____

_____

_____

_____

Secret #5 Don't Listen to Naysayers. Surround Yourself With Positive Thinkers AND Doers

It's happened to me; it's happened to you: a time when you were doing something really fulfilling and feeling fantastic about it. Suddenly, someone said something negative to or about you, or someone reprimanded and embarrassed you in front of others. In front of your boss or colleagues. Repeated verbal abuse, or the presence of negative people in your life who have stung you with their negative words and actions, can affect you for a lifetime. These people are clearly obstacles. I call them "Dream Stealers." I urge you to stand tall, face down the bullies of your soul who have thrown you off guard and are robbing you of your dreams.

There are five time-tested techniques to use when dealing with negative people:

1. **Set time boundaries.** As much as it is within your power, limit your time with them. Choose, this day, to invest your hours and days in your WHO. Your WHO friends will not demand anything of you. Remember the word "unconditional." Who do you need to draw boundaries with and why?

_____

_____

_____

2. **Guard your heart.** Let negative words and condescending looks bounce off you as if you were guarded by armor—the armor of WHO! Remember, there are other people—your WHO—who will always love you BECAUSE you are you. Who do you need to spend less time with?

_____

_____

_____

3. **Focus on the positive.** Find one good thing about them (yes, I know this will be difficult) and let your mind dwell on that one positive thing. Think of something good in that negative person at work or in your neighborhood.

Write it down and commit to reaching out in a positive way this week.

_____

_____

_____

4. **Be assertive and ask them to be more supportive.** This type of honesty may unlock the door to a better relationship, even if it is opened just a crack.

5. **Now, move on.** Move into your future with your WHO friends, who are divinely placed in your life to help you reach your highest potential.

IT'S A JOURNEY!

There may be an unfamiliar path you will need to walk to get going in the direction of your dream or a goal. There will be a few detours, pitfalls, unexpected twists and heartache along the way. But don't give up! Remember, a detour is not permanent. It's not the road to your destiny. It's a necessary but temporary side route.

There are plenty of people every day who overcome tremendous deficits and move past seemingly insurmountable obstacles to achieve greatness. That's why stories like "Tell-em Frank Beaudine from Chicago" or "June Jones entering himself into a game" are ones you'll never forget!

Perhaps there are some things you need to acquire or learn. Maybe there's someone you need to meet who holds the key to your destiny and who will help you succeed. A detour could mean you help someone else achieve their goals and in the process, discover some key elements you'll need to accomplish on your own. **Learn to view every problem you encounter as "an opportunity in disguise."** Don't get angry and don't get discouraged. Remember:

"The road to success is always under construction."

CHAPTER 8

GOING THE DISTANCE WITH YOUR WHO

"Some people enter our lives and leave almost instantly. Others stay and forge such an impression on our heart and soul that we are... forever changed."

~Author Unknown

YOU GOT WHO

Remember my WHO journey? I whittled over 5,365 contacts down to 87 WHO friends! Paring this list back rather than growing it larger, as so many do today, turned out to be not only the right decision for my business... but my life. You've also journeyed through your lists and now should have a solid WHO foundation to work from. The quantity is not really what counts; it's the quality of these WHO relationships that matters most.

You've also discovered in life that some relationships are just easier to maintain than others. There are some people you just naturally like spending time with and going deep with these friends comes easily. There are other friends you wish lived closer because you feel a deep soulful kinship would blossom into something great if you only you could spend more time together. And then, there are some friends, for a reason or a season, you just can't seem to get time to spend together because your schedules don't match up. They have boys, you have girls. They're at baseball practice and you're at dance. You want to see each other, but your lives have you going in different directions and it's just too difficult to spend face-to-face time together. Each of these kinds of friends can sometimes be labeled as "high maintenance" but, in truth, if you just understand how to attentively and genuinely care for these friends, you'll have accomplished something far greater than you ever imagined.

So how do you keep the WHO-fires burning with your friends—both near and far? It's simple—**Remember, Reach Out and Reconnect!** In this chapter, we'll explore easy ways to preserve your WHO relationships, regardless of time and distance. We'll also talk about how to cultivate your newer relationships, as well as rekindle those important friendships from the past.

BACK TO THE FUTURE. . .SORT OF

I think we all want to Reconnect with people from our past. They've been part of our lives, and, for better or worse, have helped make us who we are now. Unlike Marty McFly, however, we do not need a DeLorean to travel back to the past to influence our present and future…we just need to let our fingers do the walking.

30-SECOND VOICEMAIL

In *The Power of WHO* I told a story about one my closest friends, Cary, who calls me almost every day. If he doesn't get me on my cell phone immediately, he would always leave me a 30-second encouraging voicemail. Since then, some of my other close friends have now joined in! Now, in addition to Cary's messages, I receive voice mails and Hey Tells from Mikey V…, Tommy Z… & Jobe-Jobe. I also get text messages from BRB and Jimmy D several times weekly! It's become a WHO-fest! I can't tell you how many times these messages have brightened my day and caused me to smile. I have now saved several of them because they so moved me. From time to time, I need to replay or re-read them if I'm feeling low. You have to love people like this in a world of cynicism and negativity. Since they do this for me, I try to come up with cool messages for them. It's become somewhat of a game we play. We try to outdo each other with encouragement. We know how tough our jobs and lives can be sometimes, and just a quick 15 or 30-second message of encouragement at the right moment sure makes all the difference!

Let me ask you, **how can you say you're great friends with your friends and not communicate?** Isn't frequency a key to growing relationships? Small touches, like texts, emails, calls, handwritten notes, or Facebook messages—Like, Comment or Reshare—they all say, "I'm thinking about my friend." Add to that spending some time together, whether it's grabbing a quick cup of coffee, sharing a meal, playing golf, or going to ball games or concerts—that's what WHO friends do! When was the last time you left a WHO friend a message saying you love-em, hope they're having a great day or you're just calling to ask if there's is anything you can do for them? Think of five WHO friends you haven't chatted with or seen for a few weeks; write down their names and what you're going to suggest you do together this week.

Remember, charity begins at home! When was the last time you called your spouse on the way home from work to ask if they needed you to bring anything home? Or brought flowers or a new movie to make the night special? Let me give you a hint, if you had to think about this for more than a nanosecond, it was TOO LONG! Write down here three things you will do this week to express your love and friendship.

What about your kids? Taking them somewhere special, just the two of you? As my girls grew up, I always tried to take them individually on a business trip. Had them go to meetings where I interviewed candidates. Asked their opinion of the person. It's amazing, but they were always spot-on. They picked the person that was nicest and had the best interpersonal skills. I usually try to send a text to my three girls every morning just to ask them: "Have I told you today that I love you?" My oldest daughter, Aly, usually responds, "Oh Daddy. I love you!" My middle daughter, Jenny, says, "You just did!" My youngest daughter, Rachel,says: "No you didn't, call me and tell me!" What will you do this week for your kids, nephews, nieces or WHO friend's kids to let them know they are special? Come on now, think and be a little creative. Be specific!

_____

_____

_____

_____

_____

We each have a past in which we've shared life with people who have contributed to our life story. Each of these WHO friends is like a patch on a quilt. They hold a special meaning and unique place in our heart. These are the WHO friends that when you get together after not seeing each other for several years you exclaim, "It's as though no time has passed at all!" Oh what joy to Remember, Reach Out and Reconnect with these precious WHO friends! It always reminds me of one of my favorite quotes:

BB **"Once someone has taken a place in your heart—they never leave!"**

That's so true!

Your choice to Reconnect may be nothing more than an enjoyable walk down memory lane, or it may open a door to a present-day conversation that can help you fulfill your goals and dreams. The important thing is you are Reconnecting, getting caught up, and sharing just how much your friendship means to you. That's what "declaring" is all about! These friends need to hear you express just how much you appreciate your friendship.

Movies, songs, gifts, and even smells can invoke memories of shared experiences with a close friend. When these memories come to mind, take a few minutes to call or write a note (Facebook works) to share the moment (and probably a good laugh) with your friend. Take a minute now and jot down a few memories you want to share with a few WHO friends this week.

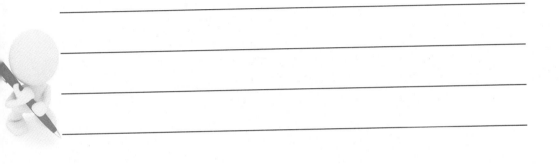

A great idea is to keep a journal by your bed. When a friend from the past comes to your mind, write down his or her name. This may be a prompt to Reach Out and Reconnect with this person. When they come to mind, don't wait — Reach Out. You never know how a word of encouragement might be a Moment Maker and just what they need to hear in their time of crisis or confusion. Remember, to have good WHO friends, you need to BE a good WHO friend. And BE is an active verb. You need to DO something!!!

If you run into an old friend while running errands, at a sporting event, concert or another friend's social gathering, be sure to ask if they have a new email address and cell number and any other new, pertinent information about them and put it in your smartphone (or on your program or beverage napkin!). Don't miss a chance to Reconnect!

It's easy to let "busyness" get in the way of Reconnecting with old friends. Therefore, it's important to seize the opportunity placed before you in a timely manner. My advice is to Reach Out within the next day! Call, email or connect through a social website to let them know how great it was to see them, or that they've been on your mind, and ask for a time to get together for lunch or coffee.

Take the initiative! Do not let negative "self-talk" deflate your desire to Reconnect with old friends. Seize the opportunity placed before you—you never know the journey that could potentially take place when your paths intersect for a second time.

TOP 10 LIST OF RECONNECTION FRIENDS

Name ten friends with whom you've fallen out of contact that you would like to Reconnect. Beside each name, write your plan for Reconnection.

1. _____

2. _____

3. _____

4. _____

5. _____

6. _____

7. _____

8. _____

9. _____

10. _____

KEEPING UP WITH YOUR LOCAL WHOS

Local and familiar WHO friends are an easier lot to keep up with, but do not take these relationships for granted. Proper care is still required to maintain great relationships.

Ever have the thought your WHO friends would probably like to know your other WHO friends? They might even be better friends but you haven't introduced them yet. You could be the catalyst to bring them together. It's a common thought we all have, but rarely act upon. Why not get several of your WHO friends together in a casual setting where they can get to know each other better? These times can be powerful beyond words.

Host a WHO party! Think of your WHO friends you think might enjoy each other's company, or may have similar interests, dreams or goals. Invite them over. You may be the link that connects two people who were meant to do business together or become close friends.

My friend Steve actually acted upon this notion a few weeks ago. He'd been thinking for some time about connecting specific friends with each other. He and his wife picked a date for a party, invited each friend or couple on their list, and to their astonishment, each not only attended, but had a wonderful time and made great new connections.

When you step out and WHO, you'll find that just one casual invitation can establish bonds of friendship that can last a lifetime. Remember the story of the mustard seed? It's the tiniest seed but it can grow into a huge tree. It only takes one WHO friend to get started in living a life full of friends. It's a win-win!

If you were to host a "WHO-Connection Party," who would be on your invite list? Neighbors, high school or college friends, people you do business with, church clubs, associations, doctor, dentist, extended family, accountant, lawyer, etc.

Write out what your invitation would say, Websites like www.evite.com and www.punchbowl.com provide invitation templates and sample wordings.

Write down a few dates for when you can host a WHO-Connection Party.

Next step: Plan your gathering and begin to make history!

Here are a few ideas that work well for me:

1. **Organize a WHO lunch or dinner at a local restaurant.** Whether with an individual WHO friend or with a few others who might enjoy each other's company, take the imitative to organize a meal together. Make sure you are thoughtful about the number of invitees and where you meet to eat. Take care to meet at a place where the noise level is ideal for conversation and be sure it's a place where everyone will be comfortable and can easily afford.

2. **Invite your WHO to a local event.** Whether a concert, ball game, or charity function, an invitation can be a perfect way to get to know a new WHO better

or show appreciation to a WHO you've known for a long time. I throw several "WHO Parties" each year for my top 30-40 local friends. One of the events is to take them to a minor league baseball game. We have a set area in left field. Hot dogs, burgers and beer. I have WHO shirts I give out. It's a blast! The agenda is to have fun together and it is never business-it's friendship time. To make sure each person is introduced, we have line-up cards that we have to to fill out like a coach. Each inning we get up and everybody sits with a different person. It's magical!

3. **Ask a WHO for help with a special project.** Your WHO wants to help you. Remember: It's a WHO Honor! If you have a special project, want help around the house, or need an extra volunteer at the homeless shelter, ask a WHO friend to help. This is how we 'do life' together! Or, maybe, you are trying to raise some money for a charity or good cause. Get your WHO friends together and make it a challenge to raise the money together. If you ask, your WHO friends will answer the call just as you are the type of WHO friend that will help them in their time of need.

I was asked by marketing guru, Kevin Kaplan, to raise money for an SMU football game against one of those non-conference, unknown teams that usually no one shows up to watch. My great WHO friends Steve Orsini and Mike Vaught, who run athletics at SMU, wanted to sell out the game for our buddy and Head Coach June Jones. How would we do that? *The Power of WHO!* We each got twelve WHO friends to get their twelve WHO friends and each agreed to raise or give $10,000! The money would go toward disadvantaged kids in Dallas who would never have the opportunity to go to a game like this.

We made it fun and did a YouTube video called "I Believe" and sold out the stadium in less than four weeks! 37,000 fans! We had a jet flyover so we could have the picture to remember that night! When I called my friends for money, I asked each for $1,000. They balked at first. They asked "What for?" I told them and they said, "No, I didn't go to SMU!" I told them they weren't giving for that reason. They were helping me, help kids and the coach I love and respect. I told them if they need help in the future I would help them. For those who gave, I'd also throw a WHO Party at my office after the season. I told them it would be worth the gift just to be with June Jones and all my other great WHO buddies! My WHO helped me raise over $20,000 in five days. That was WHO powerful!

NEAR-FAR-AND ALL POINTS IN-BETWEEN

These three things work for friends near and far.

1. **Schedule WHO conversations.** This is one of our favorites! We call it WHO Friday. From 2-4 pm on Fridays, everyone in the firm stops what they are working on and calls some people from their WHO list. Not for business, but to check in on how they are really doing. The stories of our friend's lives being changed during these calls are amazing. I bet you won't be surprised to hear that Friday has become our biggest day of business.

2. **Send birthday, anniversary and congratulatory greetings.** Thoughtfulness is silver; acting on your thoughtfulness is golden—a true treasure of the heart. There is power in the hand-written note or card (the one that actually gets mailed, that is!). Take the time to keep a calendar of your WHO friends' important dates and make the time to let them know how much you care.

3. **Send 30-second encouraging voicemails or text messages.** Think: who can I encourage today? When someone comes to your mind – perhaps you ran across a quote or a story that made you think about a WHO friend – send them a quick text, email, or voice message to let them know that you're thinking of them.

PAY IT FORWARD

When you make the extra effort to celebrate, encourage, and help others, it establishes stronger bonds of friendship. Each time you do it, you are making an investment that is never wasted. The key to investing in your friends is your willingness to be available. Being there is the essence of true friendship and is what unleashes The Power of WHO.

My great friend Tom Chenault, who is America's voice for Home Based Business Radio, always reminds me that an essential part of reaching out is also letting others reach out to you.

> **Thoughtfulness is silver; acting on your thoughtfulness is golden—a true treasure of the heart.**

I liked the movie *Yes Man*. Yes, the movie's star, Jim Carrey, goes over the top by saying "yes" to everyone in every circumstance. But, what would it look like if we took a cue from this man's same spirit of generosity by saying "yes" to our friends more often? Ask yourself: Am I a 'yes person' with my WHO friends? Before you answer, think about the last time someone asked for your help. How did you respond? Remember...**a true WHO friend will do their best to help you right now.** Your reciprocation in their time of need makes all the difference.

In today's overly busy, complex world, we fill our lives with activities and distractions that really don't matter. All the while ignoring the very things that matter most: our relationships with others. Each of us has the power to affirm our friends in ways that will bless and encourage them beyond measure. This is our real work—telling your WHO that they are a 'somebody' who matters to you!

Of the examples listed in this chapter on how to cultivate your WHO friendships, which ones stood out to you as the most doable in the next month?

What steps do you need to take to make it happen?

_____

_____

_____

_____

_____

_____

_____

Who will you send a note of encouragement to this week?

_____

_____

_____

_____

_____

_____

Who can you tell that you appreciate?

_____

_____

_____

_____

_____

_____

_____

And finally, I'm challenging you to write a simple encouraging text to your 12-3-1 Inner Circle friends today.

CHAPTER 9

THE WHO IN YOU WILL CREATE YOUR LEGACY!

"If you could only sense how important you are to the lives of those you meet; how important you can be to the people you may never even dream of. There is something of yourself that you leave at every meeting with another person."
~ Mr. Rogers

My dad was a "dreamer"—a "go for it" kind of guy. He taught me many lessons; one was the importance of seeing firsthand "how" great athletes, executives or politicians could "get themselves up" for a crucial "moment" in time.

It could be a Hail Mary throw from "Roger the Dodger" Staubach to Drew "Mr. Clutch" Pearson. It could be an inspiring speech by Steve Jobs to staff and investors to turn around Apple Computer or what happened that special day at Ground Zero when President George W. Bush grabbed the bullhorn and shouted: "I can hear you! I can hear you, the rest of the world hears you, and the people who knocked these buildings down, will hear all of us soon!" Great people somehow have this innate ability to seize "the moment." They do this by drawing the necessary energy from not just within themselves but also from people around them that believe in them. This "energy" is amazing and can create impossible feats. When delivered in the clutch, it creates a "Legacy."

ARNIE'S ARMY

My dad loved the "King of Golf" Arnold Palmer. When I was young, we used to stalk him. Okay, not really, but we were part of "Arnie's Army." Back in 1973, we went to the Bob Hope Desert Classic in Palm Springs to watch him play. I'll never forget these father/son adventures. There's nothing like being with your dad.

On the last day, Arnie was leading the tournament by one shot when he hooked his drive into the woods on the 6th hole. He and his caddie walked over to where the ball was and set the golf bag down to assess the situation. Arnie was at his peak in talent at the time and just seemed to ooze with charisma. The way he hitched his pants, tilted his head, and how he finished each tournament with a charge—he always 'wowed' the crowd.

Well, the situation wasn't good and his caddy said, "You're 248 yards to the green and to even get there you'd have to hit a miraculous shot down under several trees and around a bend to a green that's tucked tight with sand traps all around it. It's just too dangerous, Arnie, and it doesn't look like a great lie anyway."

"Hit a wedge," his caddy advised. "All we need to do is get back in the fairway and we're in business."

Did I tell you that "great people" hate to play it safe? They're just not discouraged by obstacles. What others see as an insurmountable problem, dreamers see as springboards to bigger and better opportunities. In other words, it's simply something that must be dealt with. Well, Arnie clearly thought like that!

So here we were tucked deep in the woods and my dad and I were right there next to him as he was deciding his course of action. Arnie was thinking about his situation, rattling the wedge in his bag, when he turned his head to look over at the crowd. He loved to feed off the energy of a crowd. There weren't ropes keeping fans away back then and when he caught my dad's eye as he was rattling the wedge, my dad shook his head "No" to the thought of hitting the wedge!

Startled, the caddy yelled: "I saw that! Don't listen to that man- Hit the wedge! Hit the wedge!" Arnie rattled the wedge again and sl-ow-ly he turned his head toward my dad and once again, He gave him the "No" sign! Arnie laughed out loud when he saw my dad's reaction and then walked out to the fairway to see if he could actually hit the shot my dad thought he could! He came back, hitched his pants and now started rattling the 4 wood in his bag! Sl-ow-ly he turned his head in our direction and this time my dad nods a "Yes" sign!

Well, that was all Arnie needed to see! He grabbed the 4 wood out of the bag, barked at the caddy to move away, and then hit a shot that has to go down in history. Smack! And the ball exploded low under the trees and then all of a sudden hooked left around the bend like it had a homing signal toward the pin. It missed all the traps and bounced up six feet from the pin! The crowd went nuts with cheers and applause. Arnie looked back at my dad, saluted him, and the folklore of Arnold Palmer all started that day just because of my dad!

Well… maybe Arnie did a few things on his own! But that's my story and I'm sticking with it!

The energy between two people is what makes great marriages, great organizations, great teams and pretty much everything else great. Arnie grabbed that energy, that extra juice from my dad that day. He turned it into not just a moment, but a Legacy of how he's remembered while playing the game of golf.

You have same greatness within you! It might not be in golf, but your gift in its own way is important to the world around you. We have to draw it out! It's there, I promise! It just has to be inspired, nurtured, encouraged and reminded!

What do you do to "get yourself up" for your moments? Where do you go for inspiration? Where's that place, WHO's that friend, what's that

> **Where's that place, WHO's that friend, what's that book, quote, or song that can turn a bad day into a great one?**

book, quote, or song that can turn a bad day into a great one? Finding that is crucial to your peace and balance in life. It's oxygen for your soul! It's where your energy becomes entwined with God. When someone delivers great inspiration and it's received like a precious gift, you're transformed. It's as if…God himself breathed life, hope, confidence, and perspective into your situation. In a flash, like Arnold Palmer, you're lifted above the fray to higher ground! Inspiration…I love it! All it takes is just one man or woman with courage—and everything changes! That's you I'm talking about! You're the "difference" tomorrow. I love what Don Quixote said way back in 1605: "Scorned and covered with scars, you still strove with your last ounce of courage to reach the unreachable stars; and the world was better for this!" Another great way to energize yourself is to lift up others. The best of the best know this and intentionally help and assist those around them in any way they can. They understand the principle of sowing and reaping. If you sow genuine care and attentive service into your family/friends' lives, you will continually reap a bountiful harvest. This life-strategy of "giving" is such an essential part of The Power of WHO. Once we change our paradigm from "Me first," "Me alone," and "I can do it by myself," to "How can I help you?" "What do you need?" and "Yes, I will help," then everything in our lives will change for the better.

Zig Ziglar said it best: **"You can get everything in life you want in life if you will just help enough other people get what they want."**

Make a commitment to:

• **Remember.** Start today investing in and nourishing your own personal WHO Network. You have already begun this with your lists in this workbook, but your work isn't finished here. The more you begin to walk in The Power of WHO as a way of life, the more you will remember those kind souls who have always given you favor. Remember, no one's too big or too small to be added to your list of friends.

Also take time for YOU! Your health must be taken seriously. Many times we get too busy and this is often overlooked or even dismissed. Are you exercising daily? Walking? Doing some weights? Eating right? Taking your vitamins? My WHO friend Richard Wright, who is CEO of the world-class wellness company AdvoCare, always reminds me of the importance of taking care of myself. He's educated me on taking the necessary supplements, making sure I exercise and get regular medical check-ups…. Don't let something sneak up on you because you were too busy. Be sure to tend to your health. I know multimillionaires right now who would trade you their fortunes for your good health. There's no amount of money, power or position in the world worth your health. What good is it to have millions in your bank account if you're not able to take a walk on the beach, in the park or even around the block?

If I haven't made this crystal clear by now, please allow me to state it one more time:

 the core of true success is love.

And that includes loving yourself enough to take care of yourself.

- **Reach Out.** Declare your friendships. The reason so many people are confused about who their true friends are is because they have never declared it. If you run a race for public office, you first have to declare that you are a candidate. Let people know that you are a friend and that you consider them to be a WHO in your life. Declare your candidacy for friendship. This isn't as difficult as it sounds. It may just begin with, "Hey, I just wanted to let you know that I have appreciated your friendship all of these years. You have always had my back and I thank you for it." Simple words. Small touches. Lifelong friend.

- **Reconnect.** Declaring your friendship may seem awkward at first, so let me make it easy: try starting out with your Inner Circle friends—your Top 12 WHO. Send them a *The Power of WHO* book. It's a great way to declare friendship and the same time teach them how to "WHO With YOU!" What good is it if you know The Power of WHO and have no one to WHO with? Across the nation, this is a strategy that many have told me you're using to Reconnect with your old friends. One of my WHO friends, Bob Tiede, who heads up leadership for a large international ministry, sent my book *The Power of WHO* to his top 100 WHO friends! In the inside cover he wrote: Dear ___, "You're my WHO! When I read this book, it reminded me of us! Thanks for your friendship and love all these years!" Bob feels *The Power of WHO* should be required reading for global outreach! Declaring and activating his most significant relationships by sending a book on friendship made a world of difference in his life and the lives of his friends.

> **What good is it if you know The Power of WHO and have no one to WHO with?**

Bob Tiede understood that *The Power of WHO* isn't a program to be followed; it is a revolutionary shift in the way you think and do life with friends. It's about your destiny and Reconnecting will take commitment and practice. And who knew that the bottom line to this entire equation would be love? If you haven't heard it today, let me remind you that you are loved, amazing, fabulous, and special! You make a huge difference! You're Important! You Got WHO! Now, pass it on....

MOMENT MAKING MENTORS

There are many more paths that lead to failure than there are that lead to success. Drive, determination and dedication pave the road to success. I've discovered that it's best to have help laying the bricks on your road's path. Because of their own experience in path-laying, mentors can show you how to pave your road and give you sage advice on how to keep it well-maintained. Choose your mentor(s) with care. According to a recent survey by the Center for Coaching and Mentoring, the most important characteristics of a mentor are to be:

- A role model

- A non-judgmental listener

- Available

- Honest / Provide insightful feedback

- Concerned on a personal level

- Encouraging, helping to set long-range goals

- Supportive and understanding

- A collaborator / Friend / Partner

- Confident in my abilities

- Patient

Who of your WHO do you consider to be mentors?

_____

_____

_____

_____

How has the presence of mentors in your life changed you for the better?

_____

_____

_____

What is stopping YOU from passing it on and being a mentor to someone special in your life? Someone who could benefit from your experiences is a great candidate!

PERSONAL BOARD OF DIRECTORS

Every day we read about or see on TV a host of actors, actresses, sports stars, and politicians fall prey to poor decisions that cost them their Legacy. These are smart and talented people with nothing but blue sky over their head and a life full of potential that crash and burn making bad decisions and choices. What were they thinking? Obviously, they weren't thinking or they wouldn't have made such poor choices. Where were their WHO?

I've come to believe one of the very best strategies you can implement to achieve maximum protection for yourself and your family is to create a Personal Board of Directors. Like a firewall that protects computers from destructive viruses that try to sneak in undetected and wreak havoc, you need that same protection from a trusted group of advisors. Your board will make your life much easier. They'll give instruction, caution, prudence, awareness, warning signs, encouragement, and so much more.

1. Mom/Dad/Equivalent

It's wise to have one of your board members be your mom or dad. Pick one. If, however, you're one of the many people without a healthy parent relationship or your folks have passed away, look around for a person willing and able to fill that role. It could be a grandparent, uncle, aunt, or even an older friend with whom you relate as a parent figure. Someone you respect and believe loves you unconditionally. Someone whose only agenda is your well-being and has some years of experience with you.

2. Mate

This could mean different people at different times in your life. In college, your mate could be a close friend or that "special someone." At some point, your mate could mean your spouse.

3. Best Friend

Your best friend needs to be someone who is loyal and courageous. A best friend is someone who has a special discernment about you and is available when you need them. Choose the one friend who will tell you what you truly need to hear, the thing that others wouldn't feel comfortable telling you. Best friends cut right to the bone. They nail you because they have an "All Access" pass to the backstage of your life. This may be your spouse but, in some cases, it may not. Husbands and wives are oftentimes attracted to each other because they are so different. The old adage "opposites attract" is alive and well in marriages all across the country. In these cases, a longtime friend may have a deeper understanding and influence in your choices that your wife or husband. That doesn't mean he or she isn't the number one person in your life, just that you have another special relationship that helps you get back to being YOU when you're off track.

4. Legal Counsel

You've probably already heard the old cliché many times: "The person who represents himself in legal matters has a fool for a client." Do yourself a favor, when it comes to legal matters, rely on knowledgeable experts! If you don't, you run a very high risk of embarrassing yourself and ending up with a bunch of legal knots that could cost a bundle to untangle. The principle is simple: pay a little now and avoid paying a lot later. Ask your WHO friends for a referral or recommendation of a good general practice attorney BEFORE you need one! Seek one out, have coffee, and just chat to begin building a relationship.

5. Career/Life Coach

People change jobs today on an average of seven to ten times in a lifetime. Thus, a career coach, a friend that's an executive recruiter, a top human resource executive, or a consultant in this area is a great advisor in time of need. They can help you assess the multitude of choices and possibilities available today. A wise and gifted life coach is a tremendous ally who can help keep you grounded emotionally and sometimes spiritually. This person is usually more interested in your character development. This person may assist you in identifying talents and gifts, writing "wow" résumés/cover letters, learning the art of interviewing, as well as giving tips on compensation, contracts, benefits, and branding. A good life coach knows that you may achieve great success and still derail your life because of character flaws that were left unattended. The crucial point is: it's a mistake to think you are smart enough to advise yourself in these important areas. Again, choose wisely. Pick an expert.

6. Financial Advisor

Statistics say that 90% of the country are not getting financial advice from an expert. I want to give you a DO and a DON'T. DO get with someone you trust who you know is competent in this field—someone you can rely on, who has a solid track record of success, whose integrity is impeccable, then take the time needed to get your finances on track. My friend Dave Ramsey and his entire collection of books, seminars and conferences on this subject are a must! (www.daveramsey.com)

DON'T try to do this on your own unless you're already very good at it, enjoy it, and intend to diligently spend a lot of time overseeing this strategic area of life. You'll need a strategy for employment income, savings income, and creating passive income. Get with someone you trust who you know is competent in this field—someone you can rely on, who has a solid track record of success, whose integrity is impeccable, then take the time needed to get your finances on track.

7. Spiritual Adviser

The most common definition of blindness describes a person who cannot see physically. But the word blind also means "unwilling or unable to perceive or understand." Each of us is "blind" in some things. We need a wise spiritual adviser to help bring understanding in areas of morality and ethics. In tough times, it's good to be able to talk and consider the wisdom of our spiritual adviser (pastor, priest, rabbi, or other trusted spiritual counselor).

WHAT SHOULD I LOOK FOR IN A PERSONAL BOARD OF DIRECTORS?

Your board of directors should have no agenda other than your well-being and success in life. Their yeas and nays should be based on fact, not emotion. They should be smart, savvy, discerning, loyal, truthful, genuine, loving and (at times) blunt. respectful, live lives of integrity, high moral character and ethical behavior. They should come from names on your 100 WHO list.

- Ask these special individuals if they would be willing to meet with and counsel you a few times a year, as needed, in person or by phone.

- Always seek the advice of those closest to you—your WHO! These are the people you love and who love you. You trust them because you know they have no selfish agenda. Your happiness and success are important to them.

- If you're about to make a wrong turn in life, these folks will tell you boldly of impending danger.

HUDDLE

Another great tip of protection is to go back to an old western circle the wagons approach with family and friends. In sport, it's called a huddle. It's when a team gathers together in a tight circle, to strategize, set a plan or play in motion, motivate or celebrate each other. Sometimes they hold hands, have arms around each other, or stand firmly shoulder to shoulder. It's clearly a show of unity and togetherness. It's a popular strategy for keeping opponents, fans, and the clamor that life throws at you outside your circle.

Commonly the leader of the huddle will inspire and lead their team toward a common goal or dream. But even though there is one person setting the course of action and inspiration, each and every person in that huddle matters. Each has an important role and no one person is greater or less important than the other if the goal is to be achieved.

Once the group or team understands the common goal and their particular role, they break out of the huddle and move in unison toward the line of attack. When done correctly, it's graceful, powerful, intimidating and oh so impressive.

Great teams believe in each other and in their team, regardless of the score or how much time is left on the clock! They have faith that, even in the midst of insurmountable obstacles and odds, they can still win! Why? Because there's a feeling of destiny, calling, something so much bigger than any one person on the team. When this takes place, the "huddle" itself becomes "Sacred Ground." Almost Spiritual. It's here, in one accord, that supernatural individual feats become common place from the most unlikely teammates. All to remind the "TEAM" of their destiny ahead!

> **"Huddle up" in life is a Big Thought for all of us. I believe a crucial strategy for success.**

Take a few moments and reflect on the following questions. Put your pen or pencil down and listen to yourself read each question. Then be quiet and listen. What are you telling yourself?

1. Do I "huddle?" with my own family? My friends? My co-workers?

2. Do I take time to get away from the clamor? From the noise that drowns out my peace and quiet?

3. Does everyone I work with understand our common goals? Do they believe in our ability to achieve them?

4. Does each special person in my life know and feel how important they are to me?

All great families, marriages, teams, organizations, associations, and charities "huddle!" Start Today!

BE A MOMENT MAKER!

When I was young, my dad was out of work for eight long months. Each day, he'd get dressed in a suit to head to the office. (At least that's what I thought he did.) When we finally went off to school, he'd circle back home to look for a job. He just couldn't bear for us to be worried; it was a different generation. Years later, when I worked with my dad in executive recruiting, if someone came in looking for a job unannounced, without an appointment, we'd always treat them like they already had one, get them a cup of coffee, because my dad taught us how lonely and vulnerable it felt to be out of work. He always told me, **"There's something great in everyone, Bob, it's your job to find it!"**

Most people can recall that one special person who took the time to invest in them and it turned their life around for the better. When someone you admire and respect believes in you, it changes everything. In the same way, there are people who look up to you. You have the key to unleash The Power of WHO to your family's and friends' dreams and goals by just believing in them and letting them know it. When you invest your life in others, it establishes a bond of friendship that's beyond measure. Each time you celebrate, encourage or help them, it's an investment that's never wasted. Our greatest opportunity to build these relationships is when someone is in a crisis. Most people want to stand clear; my advice—jump in and help!

What an amazing truth: "there's something great in each of us!" It's my message to you today. You're a treasure chest of gifts and talents! Don't let anyone tell you differently! In fact, you do one thing, some one thing, better than anyone in the world and yet you might not have let that gift out of the bag yet.

Recording artist Nichole Nordeman's song "Legacy" succinctly speaks to the internal question we all ask in the midst of our life's journey: "How will they remember me?"

I won't lie, it feels alright to see your name in lights
    We all need an 'Atta boy' or 'Atta girl'

But in the end I'd like to hang my hat on more besides
    The temporary trappings of this world
I want to leave a legacy
    How will they remember me?
Did I choose to love?
    Did I point to You enough?
I want to make a mark on things
    I want to leave an offering . . .

The greatest potential you have to improve your life is hidden right now within the relationships you've already been given. Don't miss this! Yes, you're going to meet great people along the path ahead and yes, they're going to be amazing, some more impactful than you could ever have dreamed! But please... don't miss today! Don't neglect your diamonds, the treasures you have!

In *Field of Dreams*, the voice whispered: "If you build it, they will come." When I first heard that, I heard within me a message about not just the importance of friends but the incredible value of the Legacy of friends. I thought about how I could build, activate, invest, empower and start doing life with these special WHO people. Too many get caught up in the WHAT in life and neglect their WHO. They are so focused on their own goals they neglect their buddies, pals, and loved ones. Instead, they live a life of "crowded loneliness." Don't let that be you! Start back today! Mitch Albom said: **"Build a little community of those you love and who love you."** Living The Power of WHO begins with how you want to be remembered.

CHAPTER 10

HOW COULD WE HAVE MISSED IT?

"Eliminate all other factors, and the one which remains must be the truth."

~Sherlock Holmes

Sherlock Holmes became world famous for his uncanny ability to perceive clues. He saw what others couldn't until he pointed them out. This remarkable gift of "seeing" most often revealed clues hidden in plain sight. You and I need the ability to detect the clues life sets before us. They're actually easy to see, but, as you and I know, we often miss the obvious.

If you were in a game but couldn't see who you were playing, that would be a distinct advantage for the other side wouldn't it? In fact, if you never were handed the "rules of the game," and the other side was, you would call a "foul" wouldn't you? Let's go one step further, if you never knew or never heard that there was a game being played, then you would likely join the ranks of millions of people who haven't seen the ball since the kick off! Why go there?

My friend, there is more than a game going on; it is a Battle and it's going on *right now*! It's happening all around us! Why not join the minority who recognize their obvious need for help and ask your WHO to help guide you through this impossible life we live. This workbook is my "Cry-Out," "My Call" to you, to help you escape from The Matrix and get back on the path you were called and destined to follow, a path of fulfillment derived from doing significant things at work and with your WHO friends!

As you recall, Neo is the main character in the movie *The Matrix*. He's connected to the "grid," unaware that he's going through life asleep. After being awakened and disconnected from the "grid" through a bizarre set of circumstances, he's faced with a whole new reality that he didn't even know existed. This new reality leads him into his destiny. The story of *The Matrix* is, in many ways, an allegory of the world we live in today. The really scary thought is that you're connected to the "grid," performing a function that doesn't utilize your gifts and talents. You're simply doing what you've been programmed to do. But you know it's not who you *really* are. Like Neo, you have to bust out. Instinctively, you know the pathway to your destiny. Your purpose lies beyond your ability to see from where you are right now. It's going to take considerable faith and courage to disconnect from the "grid", which is your "real" world, and follow your recurring dream. Are you stuck to the "grid?" Do you see the consequences for you and your family if you stay hopelessly attached?

> **A recent Gallup Poll states that 80% of those working in a corporation are not using their #1 talent.**

Did I hear you just say, "Now Bob, that's just conspiracy thinking?" Really? Let's look at some statistics.

Millions of people are out of work. And millions more are under-employed or really unhappy in their current job. Who are these people? Do we care? Of course we do! They're our friends, neighbors, and family. They've been told the answer to finding their dream job is to go online, get in line, fill out this, fill out that for people they don't know and who don't know them. As Dr. Phil says, "How's that working out for them?"

The strategy we've been taught in college, seminars, conferences, books and even our places of worship is that whatever it is you need, if you don't have the answer—try something called "networking." "Networking?" What does that mean really? Well, unfortunately, when you read the fine print it means endless visits to faceless websites, handing out business cards to strangers at business conferences, going to networking meetings and sending executive recruiters and Human Resource executives; "Dear Sir", "To Whom it May Concern", and "Dear Recruiter" letters! "Dear Recruiter", that's an oxymoron, isn't it?

A recent Gallup Poll states that 80% of those working in a corporation are not using their #1 talent. Wow! That means we are spending billions of dollars training and developing people for jobs they don't want to do and are not really qualified to do anyway.

- **69%** of those who have a job believe that: "A bad day at the beach is better than a good day at work!"

- Over **50%** of all college grads can't find a job. Yikes, I thought that was an inalienable right. Why would anybody spend all that money for a college education, if they knew they were going to get just any job rather than a dream job? A job they could actually ENJOY and apply their unique gifts and talents? Worse yet, why would anybody in their right mind GO INTO DEBT to earn a worthless degree?

In another survey, a research team from Harvard University polled 12,000 full-time employees and asked them about their feelings at work. In one-third of the 12,000 replies, the workers reported feeling unhappy and unmotivated. They expressed "frustration," "disdain" or "disgust" with their jobs. And do you think America's executives and managers have a clue what to do? Not! The same researchers state, "95% of managers failed to recognize that progress in meaningful work is the primary motivator, well ahead of traditional incentives like raises and bonuses."

Why is this happening? Is there possibly a correlation between satisfaction at work and friendship? The answer is yes! It is found in a great book called *Vital Friends*, by bestselling author Tom Rath, formerly with Gallup. Tom conducted a study and found only **18% of companies today provide opportunities for "friendship" on the job. That means that 82% don't?** It is startling to think that 82% of the people surveyed still believe that old concept that "friendship and business are taboo." That "fraternizing with friends at work" is not desired. In fact, just go to your cubicle and work! I can almost hear someone say: "Let's keep work, recreation and time with friends separate. Ok?" What? Like we're supposed to enjoy going to work every day with people we don't know and don't trust? That doesn't make sense!

On the other hand, is having friends at work a good idea for companies today? Yes! The study found that **if you had just one true friend, just one in your organization, you were 40% more productive in your role. 40 percent, WOW!** With one friend at work, they found that you'll engage more with customers, get more done, have more fun at work, have fewer accidents, share more ideas, and feel your opinion counts. That should be front page news! I think every company would like to have 40% more productivity from their employees! Wouldn't they? And it gets even better. . . if you have three true friends at work, the study says you'll have a 96% percent chance of having a satisfying life—not just a job! That would cut employee turnover across the country significantly. But that's not happening. Unfortunately, only 30 % of workers have one friend at their job. No wonder there's so much stress in the workplace.

Listen to a recent NY Times article: **"The Gallup-Healthways Well-Being Index, which has been polling over 1,000 adults every day since January 2008, shows that Americans now feel worse about their jobs – and work environments – than ever before. And that's people who have a job! Gallup estimates the cost of America's disengagement crisis at a staggering $300 billion in lost productivity annually."**

And this dissatisfaction in the workplace is bubbling over on the home front. After a long day's work, people are getting in planes, trains and automobiles frustrated that they're being tolerated at work as opposed to appreciated and celebrated. By the time they get home, they've joined Saturday Night Live's "Whiner Family," complaining about the day, the pay, let alone the "way." After a while, doing a job you detest with people that clearly don't care about you—gets old! No wonder the worst statistic of all, and the one that has the single biggest impact on our life and those we love, is that nearly 60% of marriages end up in divorce. And it doesn't stop there. Today's new normal "family" is primarily a single, working mom with a couple of kids. Families with a dad and mom living under the same roof with their kids are the minority now!

Another favorite movie scene of mine is from *Joe Versus the Volcano*, starring Tom Hanks. Joe has a terrible job and a despicable boss. He's become a hypochondriac, anesthetized to the whole meaning of life, and feels he's lost his soul. He quits his job and takes off on a wild adventure where he meets up with Patricia, played by Meg Ryan. The two are having a discussion about life and beliefs when she says this amazing line to Joe: "My father says that almost the whole world is asleep. Everybody you know. Everybody you see. Everybody you talk to. He says that **only a few people are awake, and they live in a state of constant, total amazement."**

That line hit me hard! Asleep! That's so true. Like those zombies in the old horror movie, *Night of the Living Dead*, he's saying that most people are just moving around but not really alive. People who "sleepwalk" through life are lethargic and have no goals because they've allowed their dreams to be pushed down by others and forgotten. They're performing functions that have no productive purpose. There's activity but no reason for it.

Are you starting to see a pattern here? How did we miss it? Why are we told from an early age, "Get a Job!" "Do it alone!" When that never works and it never has.

If I'm trying to beat you in a game, wouldn't it be a great strategy to get you alone, isolated? That's what the great quarterbacks do all the time. They call a play to isolate a defensive player in coverage, fool the whole defense into believing they are going to run and then, BAM, there's a guy dancing in the end zone behind the secondary after he scored. The crazy thing is, the quarterback will keep doing it, over and over again until the defense realizes what's happening to them and changes their strategy. When we feel caught in this trap, we need a time-out and a new strategy.

Wasn't life meant to be simpler than what we've made of it?

Many of us are working way too hard in jobs we don't like while pursuing relationships that are actually bad for us and in some cases even living in places we don't enjoy. We're fooled into pursuing position, power, and money, having been told it will bring us the true treasures of peace, happiness, and a deep-down contentment—but it doesn't. The world will distract you. If you're not careful, you will actually forget who you are and end up settling, putting your dreams and goals on hold.

Have you settled for a counterfeit destiny?

It's time to press the RESET button in our lives. It's time to remember who we are, where we want to be going, how we want to get there and WHO we want to get there with. It's time to get started.......

WHO GROUPS

What if you started a local WHO group next week? You got together weekly with your three closest friends for the sole purpose of helping each other develop plans to achieve your goals, live your dreams, and work through your current crises? I'm not talking about meeting new friends or people you don't know, I'm talking about getting together with three WHO friends, buddies or close friends who actually care about you and who would feel that seeing you weekly is "normal." Over time the goal is to have twelve. But to start, just get your three and set a time next week to meet together for an hour or so.

What if the combined experience of these three, plus the power of each and everyone's circle of influence, could open up doors and opportunities that you never imagined possible? That would be a great idea wouldn't it? Of course it would. But does anyone do this? No! Instead we go to "networking meetings," get on monster.com, match.com, whatever.com and attend home church groups based on zip codes rather than at friends' homes. Big Mistake. What are we thinking? ARE we thinking?

I received a call recently from a friend of the family. He had been with the same company for twenty-eight years. Due to the downturn in the economy, he was asked to take an early retirement. So he joined a local networking group. Not knowing what to expect, he soon discovered that he didn't like it at all. He described it as a group of people who had no connection, forced to sit in pairs and talk about issues and problems in each other's lives. The whole experience was just one notch above a sharp stick in the eye. He asked me, "Bob, what do I do? I have to work. I still have kids going to college, and one of my two girls is engaged to be married. I've forgotten how one looks for a job. It's almost like dating again, and I've forgotten how to court. I feel paralyzed."

I asked my friend if he had developed any sort of plan. He looked at me like a deer in the headlights and spoke some unintelligible gibberish. Worst of all, he was actually thinking of sending out mass e-mail blasts to a bunch of people he didn't even know. He was clearly panicked. He had absolutely no clue what to do. My heart went out to this man whom I had known and respected for years. His world had been turned upside down, and he just needed a WHO friend to put a firm hand on his shoulder and help stabilize him. He needed a WHO group but didn't have one to go to.

Kevin Spacey starred in a motion picture called *Pay It Forward*, playing a high school teacher who assigned each student in his class to think of a way to make a significant impact in the lives of others. He challenged them to come up with ideas on how their class could change the world for the better. One of the students presented a simple, yet profound idea that required everyone in the class to perform three unconditional acts of kindness for a total stranger with the only stipulation being that the recipient would go and do the same thing for three other people. The concept was to "pay it forward," thereby creating an exponential effect that would change the world for the better.

I loved that story. But doing this for strangers is hard to sustain. Wouldn't it be so much easier if you knew the person to whom you were giving a reference, endorsement and testimonial? Think about it. If you have minor surgery and you're discharged, who do you call to come get you—people you know or people you don't know? Of course, you call people you know!

- When a new basketball or football coach takes over, who do they bring with them?

- When a new CEO arrives, who do you think they recruit as part of the new management team?

- In Washington, when an administration changes, who joins the new president?

In all cases its people they already know or know of through friends. People they can trust from day one because they have a relationship and shared experience.

So, let give me you one final example why WHO matters more than WHAT. Over the last thirty years, I've sat in on countless interviews with CEOs and top hiring managers watching their response to each candidate's pitch. I've discovered there are four things a CEO thinks about when they first meet each candidate.

Interestingly, these are also the same questions everyone thinks! It's a hierarchy of thought.

1. Do I know you?
2. Do I like you?
3. Do you understand my needs?
4. Are you the best solution for me?

Given this hierarchy, where do people feel most comfortable starting? Do they go to the top and build a relationship? No, we've been taught to sell our WHAT rather than our WHO. So out come the business cards, PowerPoint's, brochures and resumes. Ugh! This, of course, doesn't work. So they move up the ladder and try to tell the CEO or hiring manager from HR that they understand their needs. What? You've been in the interview for fifteen minutes and you understand their needs? Really?

Let me ask you a question. Do you normally share your needs with total strangers? Of course not! And neither does a CEO! So get ready, coming fast behind is normally the sales pitch, what I call the pick-up lines people give at bars. Why? They've been taught they can "wow" a person with their personality and charm. But this is tougher than they think. Since the meeting is won or lost in the first five minutes; it's extremely hard to establish the necessary "trust" in that short period of time. So what makes the difference? The secret is being known before you even walk in the room. If someone the CEO knows and trusts recommended you, things will go much more smoothly. And who is that "someone'? Hello! It will more than likely be a mutual friend!

Over 80% of all job placements happen this way. It's the same when trying to win a piece of business. We just don't want to admit it. Whenever I ask someone, "How did you get that cool job?" they say, "Well, my best friend introduced me to this person and it was magic" or "I could never have gotten on this board or gotten this piece of business without the help of my great friend and mentor." Friends are the key! Friends you have known for a long time. Friends are people who love you and who know your character, integrity and work ethic. Friends are people who want to help you achieve your goals and live your dreams. Wouldn't you work harder for a friend who went out of the way to get you an opportunity? Of course you would!

But today even though getting opportunities through friends is actually the norm, it's been hidden. In fact, when this subject is talked about out in the open there is this kind of "taboo" tied to it. Like you got a favor, cheated, or you used your influence and somehow that's BAD. No, that's ridiculous!

I was recently in Alaska with my great WHO friends Jim McMahan and Stewart Hunter. We had a great week in the wilds, sharing stories, dreams and life's challenges. Getting quiet with your soul allows you to hear and see things far greater than you could ever imagine. While we were there, we caught a 200 lb. halibut and some huge silver salmon, saw sea lions and whales jumping close by, and still we wanted more. I turned to Jim and asked, "Where are all the Bald Eagles? Isn't this the place you're supposed to see these amazing birds?" Jim grabbed his binoculars and BAM, there they were! The crazy thing was they were there all the time. We just missed them perched right there in the trees. Gorgeous! Majestic! It reminded me what Thomas Carlyle once said: "The eye sees what it brings the power to see."

I started *The Power of WHO* with one main thought that I want to leave you with:

"You Already Know Everyone You Need To Know!"

Your diamonds are already in your backyard. All you have to do is **Remember, Reach Out and Reconnect!** Decide to make friendship a priority.

WHO knows where this life may lead you?

Voice Your Dreams!

"Every person has a seed of greatness within them! YOU do! Something so amazing, so big! But we have to get that which is within each of us out for all the world to see!" ~Bob Beaudine

I never knew how important a "Notes" section at the end of a book was until I looked back at all the books I read and loved over the years and saw my scribbled notes in the margins. Sure would have been easier if the authors had given me some blank pages to record my thoughts!

With this in mind, I added this Notes section here for you! These pages are for your thoughts and your dreams. They will make it YOUR book. So dream out loud!

Why do this? Because we tend to forget. If you don't journal your thoughts when you get them, you just might forget that one person you were meant to call or that one idea that was meant for you that could change the entire trajectory of your life! All my scribbles over the years inspired me to write *The Power of WHO*. Just think what's in you!

At the top of each page of notes I am going to give you one of my favorite quotes to inspire you to be YOU!

"Each day is a spectacular opportunity, a whole new canvas for you to paint upon." —Martha Beaudine

"To understand the heart & mind of a person, look not at what they achieved, but what they aspire to do."
—Khalil Gibran

"As you reach for understanding, you find that your ladder of facts is not long enough...and you go get a ladder of faith."
—Robert Brault

*"Hope is a good thing, maybe the best of things,
and no good thing ever dies."*
—from the movie Shawshank Redemption

_____

_____

_____

_____

_____

_____

_____

_____

_____

_____

_____

_____

_____

"What we need are more people that specialize in the impossible!"
—Theodore Roethke

"Even after all this time, the Sun never says to the Earth 'You owe me.' With a 'love' like that, it lights up the whole sky!"
—Hafiz of Sharaz

_____

_____

_____

_____

_____

_____

_____

_____

_____

_____

_____

_____

_____

_____

"If we did all the things we were capable of doing, we would astonish ourselves." —Thomas Edison

"Son, when you were born, you cried while the world rejoiced! Live your life in such a way that when you die the world cries while you rejoice." —Robin Sharma

_____

_____

_____

_____

_____

_____

_____

_____

_____

_____

_____

_____

_____

"The real voyage of discovery consists not in seeing new landscapes, but in having new eyes." —Marcel Proust

"When was the last time you woke up and realized that today could be the best day of your life? Participate in your dreams today. There are unlimited opportunities available with this new day. Take action on those wonderful dreams you've had in your mind for so long." —Steve Maraboli

THE POWER OF WHO!

You Already Know Everyone You Need To Know

Bob Beaudine, CEO of Eastman & Beaudine, manages the nation's leading executive search firm in sports, entertainment and business. He is a dynamic, engaging speaker who vibrantly speaks to companies, industry associations, colleges and universities on a multitude of topics including *The Power of WHO!*.

Sports Illustrated recently named Bob the "Top Front Office Matchmaker in Sports." The Wall Street Journal named Bob's firm the "Top Executive Recruiting Firm in College Sports."

For media inquiries or booking information please call Katy at 972-312-1012 or visit Eastman-Beaudine.com.